TELEWORK

a critical component
of your total rewards strategy

About WorldatWork®

WorldatWork (www.worldatwork.org) is the association for human resources professionals focused on attracting, motivating and retaining employees. Founded in 1955, WorldatWork provides practitioners with knowledge leadership to effectively implement total rewards— compensation, benefits, work-life, performance and recognition, development and career opportunities—by connecting employee engagement to business performance. WorldatWork supports its 30,000 members and customers in 30 countries with thought leadership, education, publications, research and certification.

The WorldatWork group of registered marks includes: WorldatWork®, workspan®, Certified Compensation Professional or CCP®, Certified Benefits Professional® or CBP, Global Remuneration Professional or GRP®, Work-Life Certified Professional or WLCP™, WorldatWork Society of Certified Professionals®, and Alliance for Work-Life Progress® or AWLP®.

WorldatWork Journal, WorldatWork Press and Telework Advisory Group are part of the WorldatWork family.

WorldatWork.
The Total Rewards Association

www.worldatwork.org

©2007 WorldatWork Press
ISBN 978-157963-171-0

Editor: Robert King
Cover Design: Melissa Neubauer
Graphic Design: Alan Luu
Production Manager: Rebecca Williams Ficker

Acknowledgements

WorldatWork would like to thank the following individuals
for their contributions to this book:

Steve Constantin, Ph.D., CCP

Nancy deLay, Ph.D., Kenexa

Sarah Flannery, Thompson Hine LLP

Gil Gordon, Gil Gordon Associates

Robert Smith, NetSmith Services

Robert Trenck, AgilQuest Corp.

Jennifer Verive, Ph.D., White Rabbit Virtual Inc.

John Vivadelli, AgilQuest Corp.

Table of Contents

Chapter 1

Fitting Telework into the Total Rewards Strategy

Until the late 20th century, almost everyone was required to go to a specific location to do their work. Jobs were determined by where employees went to get work done, be it a store, farm, factory or office. However, technological and other developments in the past 30 years have resulted in important changes for millions of people, so that work today is less often characterized by traveling to a single, primary location. As *BusinessWeek* (2006) put it: "Work is no longer a place where you go, but something you do."

The use of the Internet and the development of mobile telephones drove most of this change. A Jan. 25, 2006, report in *The Economist* documents the development when it notes,

> More people have adopted the Internet and mobile telephony more quickly than any other technologies in history. By the end of last year 1 billion people were on the Internet, while the number of mobile phone users was at least 1.5 billion. (Wolf 2006)

Telework Defined

Whether one uses the words telework, telecommuting, virtual work, mobile work, distributed work or eWork, people are increasingly able to work from anywhere. For the purposes of this book, however, there are two definitions to keep in mind:

- *Telecommute* is defined as periodically or regularly performing work for one's employer from home.
- *Telework* is defined as performing all of one's work from any remote location

either from an outside employer or through self-employment.

The terms "telework" and "telecommute" often are used interchangeably, and while many people use them for different situations, what they have in common is the idea of decentralizing the office and enabling the performance of "office work" away from the traditional office location.

In the "Telework Trendlines for 2006" report from WorldatWork and conducted by The Dieringer Research Group, the home was the most prevalent away-from-the-office work location cited, but other locations were used as well. The survey found that:

- 28.7 million people worked at home at least one day a month.
- 24.6 million worked at a customer or client's place of business.
- 24.1 million worked in the car.
- 20.3 million worked in cafes and restaurants.

The report also indicated that the number of Americans whose employers allow them to work from home at least one day per month increased to 12.4 million in 2006, up from approximately 9.9 million in 2005. (WorldatWork 2007) Appendix A provides the full "Telework Trendlines for 2006" report.

Working from anywhere is, in part, in response to global working conditions reported by the U.N. International Labour Organization study, *Decent Working Time: New Trends, New Issues.*

> Today's world of work is characterized by 'atypical and unpre-
> dictable' work hours, with intense competition driving companies
> to tailor their work more and more closely to market demands.
> The result is hours that are variable and unpredictable, and an
> increase in weekend and night work. (WFC Resources 2006)

However, people increasingly want the flexibility to work from anywhere also to meet their demanding personal and family needs. Telework helps employees achieve a work-life balance while also responding to the competitive market demands confronting their employers.

A 2001 study of IBM employees by Brigham Young University researchers showed that workers who believe they have flexibility can work eight hours more a week and still feel they have work-life balance. (Alliance for Work-Life Progress 2005a) This suggests that telework can more effectively meet the needs of the employee and the employer alike.

The option to work from home, satellite offices and other locations is becoming part of standard operating procedures in most companies, according to a survey conducted by Yoh, a talent and outsourcing services provider.

Yoh surveyed 198 HR managers at the Society for Human Resource Management Conference and Exposition in June 2006 about their companies' telework policies. The survey found 81 percent of hiring managers have policies allowing employees to work remotely. Moreover, 67 percent of hiring managers believe the number of employees who work remotely will likely increase during the next two years.

Telework as a Total Rewards Tactic

Telework fits within the work-life element of the Total Rewards Model to attract, retain and motivate employees. (See Figure 1-1.) Telework may be the most flexible of flexible work options available in work-life for employees and employers, and telework is well suited to help companies effectively compete in the global, highly technological and fast-changing conditions of the 21st century.

Attract

The attractiveness of telework for the employer depends, in part, on the type of work an enterprise engages in, the jobs that are available, the community where the organization is located and the demographics of potential employees.

For technology-based companies, telework is becoming more common as firms with solid telework programs are the epitome of the 21st century fast-paced global

Figure 1-1
Telework and the Total Rewards Model

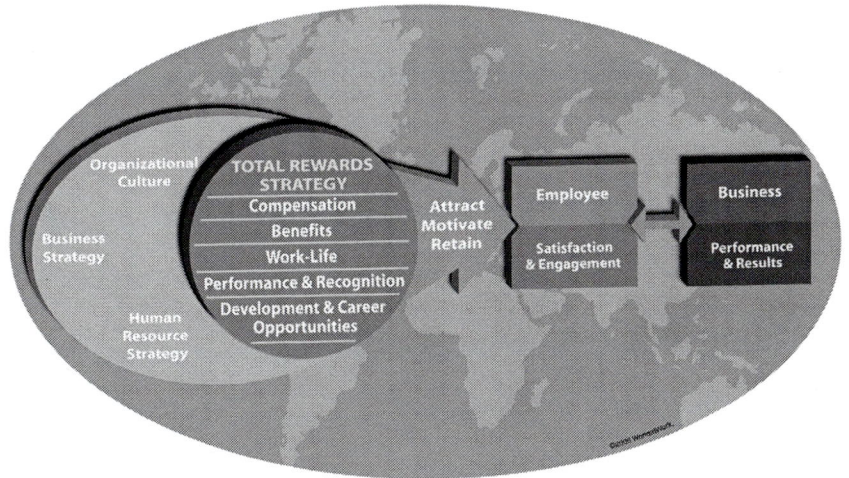

firm. Further, these firms employ people who are comfortable with the computer and communications technologies that make telework possible today. Sun Microsystems is a perfect example: About 40 percent of its worldwide employees participate in its iWork program. Since 1996, the iWork program has allowed employees to work from anywhere in the world, which means the company has great flexibility in getting talent wherever it can, according to Eric Richert, vice president of open work solutions. (WFC Resources 2006) In addition, *BusinessWeek* (2006) reports,

> Sun Microsystems Inc. calculates that it's saved $400 million over six years in real estate costs by allowing nearly half of all employees to work anywhere they want. And this trend seems to have legs. A recent Boston Consulting Group study found that 85 percent of executives expect a big rise in the number of unleashed workers over the next five years. In fact, at many companies the most innovative new product may be the structure of the workplace itself.

Further, certain jobs lend themselves to a work-from-anywhere arrangement, such as sales positions and customer service. In sales, employees are frequently "out of the office" to meet with current and prospective clients. Being in the office is rare for a successful sales person. Advances in computer and communications technologies mean that customer service can be successfully delivered by employees from anywhere, including their homes.

Generally, telework is well suited for any kind of knowledge-related position, whatever the nature of an employer's work. As long as connecting to people via communications technologies or computers is effective for conducting business, telework is a viable option for both employers and employees for at least part of the work week.

Some metropolitan areas have high traffic congestion or real estate costs that might not appeal to some people. This also is true of a job opportunity that requires relocation. In addition, for family or other personal reasons, a prospective employee may not want or be able to leave his or her home. Telework gives companies access to a broader employment pool—one not restricted by geography—thus improving a firm's chances to attract the most qualified personnel without facing extraordinary recruiting costs.

The flexibility that telework provides is appealing in different ways to different segments of the workforce. In a 2006 survey conducted by Monster.com, 41 percent of women and 26 percent of men reported believing that having no flexibility with regard to work hours is a reason not to accept a new position. Further, many Generation Y employees (born between 1978 and 1989) expect access to technology tools allowing them to work from anywhere. Many of this 31 million-plus population already are or will be seeking employers that give them the flexibility they have grown up with at home and in their schools and colleges.

An earlier study in 2000 by the Radcliff Public Policy Center showed men were interested in more flexibility. The survey reported that many of the 1,008 male workers surveyed between the ages of 20 and 39 indicated that spending more time with their families was more important to them than challenging work or earning a high salary. Seventy percent of respondents indicated a willingness to give up some pay in exchange for more family time. (Alliance for Work Life Progress 2005b)

Increasingly, evidence shows that the flexibility telework can offer is appealing to more people in the workforce. And as a result, firms offering such flexibility have a larger pool from which to attract new employees.

Motivate

A Gallup study found that "remote workers are more likely to be engaged than those around the office. Twenty eight percent of people who work from home, 35 percent of 'road warriors' (people whose jobs require constant travel), and 39 percent of sales representatives are engaged." At the same time "only 25 percent of people who work primarily in an office setting are engaged." (Robison 2006)

Insurance provider Aetna has documented the engagement benefits of telework. It began its formal telework program in 2004. From 2004 to 2006, Aetna measured employee satisfaction, productivity and effectiveness. Its analysis showed that telework improves employee satisfaction and loyalty and, as a result, productivity of teleworkers is 7 percent higher on average than in-office employees. (See Figures 1-2 and 1-3 on pages 6 and 7.) (Brostek 2006a)

Retain

Telework also has proven to be an effective retention tool for employees. At AT&T, executives say one-half of employees who telework and received job offers from competitors said they stayed with AT&T because the company allows them to work from home. (WFC Resources 2006)

Aetna not only found that its telework program helped attract new employees, but also retain them. (See Figure 1-4 on page 8.) In 2005, telework employees had an attrition rate of 7.02 percent, while similar office workers had an attrition rate of 14.88 percent. (Brostek 2006b)

Cendant Mobility reduced its voluntary turnover in 2000 from more than 19

Figure 1-2

Telework's Effect on Employee Satisfaction and Loyalty at Aetna

Employee survey results indicate that telework improves employee satisfaction and loyalty, especially survey items related to employee engagement, job satisfaction and work-life balance. (Brostek 2006a)

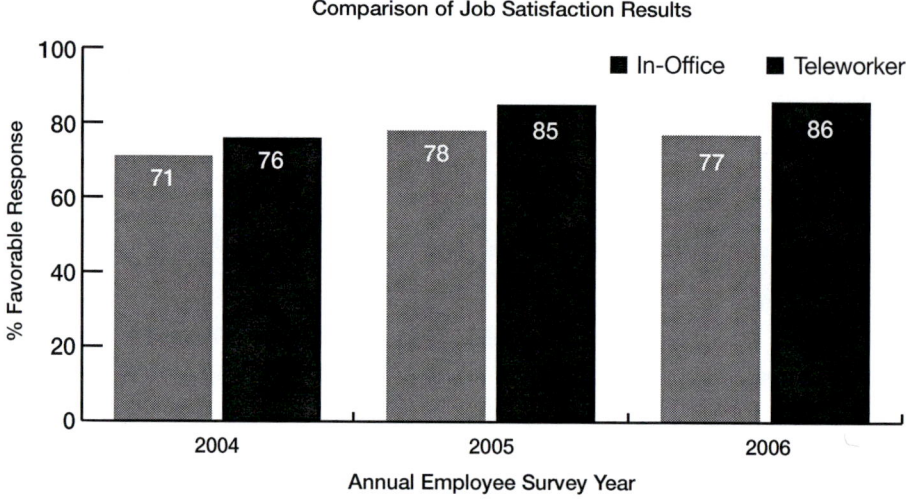

Comparison of Job Satisfaction Results

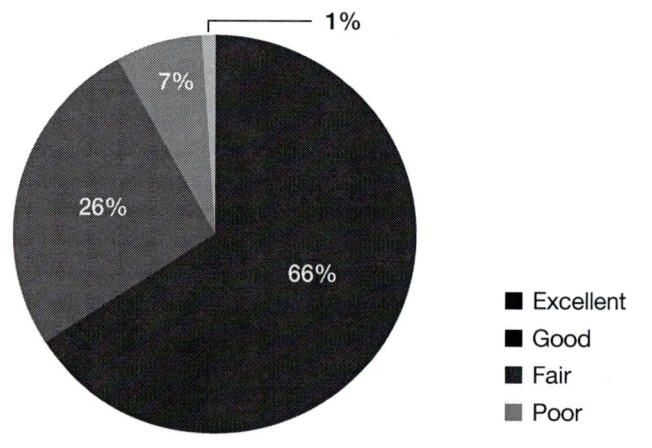

How would you rate your work-life balance since moving to a telework arrangement?

Figure 1-3

Teleworker Productivity at Aetna

A productivity and effectiveness study at Aetna showed that teleworker scorecard ratings average higher than in-office employees. (Brostek 2006a)

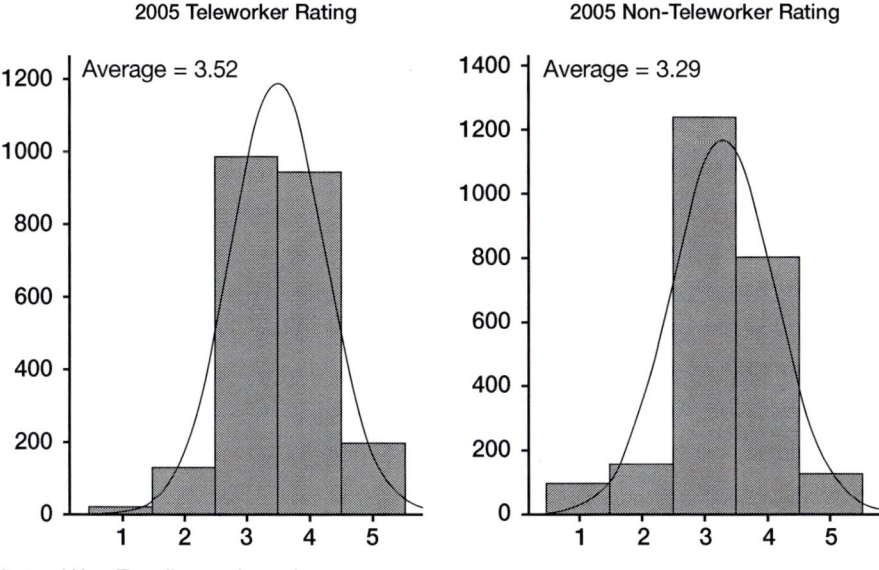

2005 Teleworker Rating — Average = 3.52

2005 Non-Teleworker Rating — Average = 3.29

Aetna Way Excellence Awards

- Five of the 32 Gold Award winners (16%) in 2005 were teleworkers.

- Four of the 10 Platinum Award Winners (40%) in 2005 were teleworkers.

percent to less than 7 percent in 2003 by implementing its Flexible Work Options that include telework. For this firm, every 1-percent reduction in turnover has resulted in at least $1 million in savings in recruitment, hiring, orientation, training, learning curve and lost productivity. (Cendant 2005)

THOR, an online travel agency, saw its turnover rate plummet from 45 percent to 3 percent after implementing a telework program. (Crane 2003)

In addition, teleworkers at Eli Lilly & Co. were more satisfied with their supervisors than non-teleworkers, a key indicator of intention to stay at the organization. (DeLay and LoVerde 2003)

Best Buy is one of telework's outstanding examples with its ROWE (results-only work environment). *BusinessWeek* (2006) reports the company's average voluntary turnover "has fallen drastically" and further reports,

... that productivity is up an average 35 percent in departments that have switched to ROWE. Employee engagement, which measures employee satisfaction and is often a barometer for retention, is way up too, according to the Gallup Organization, which audits corporate cultures ... By letting people work off-campus, Best Buy figures it can reduce the need for corporate office space, perhaps rent out the empty cubicles to other companies and plow the millions of dollars in savings into its service initiative.

Telework also may have a strong influence in the retention of a company's more senior workers who are approaching retirement. The potential labor shortage, particularly with the impending retirement of baby boomers, is an issue that was touched on in a presentation at the 2006 Telework Conference. Joel Ratekin, Director of Corporate Real Estate and Workplace Strategy, Capital One, noted that the United States is facing a future talent shortage. Ratekin indicated:

- By 2006, two workers will exit the workforce for every one entering.
- The 25- to 44-year-old age group will decline by 15 percent during the next 15 years.
- By 2008, a shortage of 10 million workers will evolve across all employment categories.

Figure 1-4
Telework as a Retention Tool at Aetna

Aetna continues to experience lower attrition rates in business units in which telework has been embraced. (Brostek 2006b)

- In 2005, non-exempt employees in the Customer Service and Claims job functions had an attrition rate of 7.02% for telework employees versus 14.88% for in-office workers.

- Patient Management Nurses in the Southeast and Southwest regions continue to see a decline in voluntary terminations.

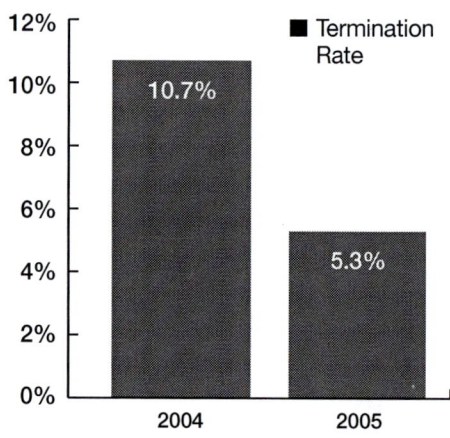

- Demand for skilled talent will grow each year until 2020.

The Sloan Center for Flexible Work Options and Older Workers at Boston College indicates that businesses responding to the needs and preferences of older workers include telework in their list of retention tools.

> Older workers may prefer to work from a different worksite, often-times because they want to reduce commuting time. Telework options enable employees to work from off-site locations (most often the employees' homes). A few workplaces allow workers to periodically switch locations, sometimes on a seasonal basis.
>
> Borders Group, which includes the Borders retail book stores, has instituted a 'passport' program enabling employees to work at more than a single location during a year. This flexibility can work well for older workers who live for part of the year in one home and reside in a different location for the remaining months but who want to maintain steady employment with a particular company. CVS and Home Depot have adopted similar practices. (Fetterman 2005 and Freudenheim 2005)

In today's job market, where work flexibility is highly valued by many in the work-force, telework is a critical tactic for attracting, motivating and retaining employees.

Chapter 2

Organizational Benefits of Telework: Beyond Total Rewards

Chapter 1 has established that telework is a powerful employer tactic to attract, motivate and retain employees. However, other important telework benefits can yield significant operating cost savings and improve overall productivity for private and public sector organizations. These benefits explain the full value telework can provide organizations to help them succeed in the 21st century.

Efficient Office Space Utilization

Whether it is a workstation, a private office with a window, or a conference room, most spaces in traditional offices are drastically underused. Numerous studies show that the average workspace utilization for commercial space in the United States and Europe between 8 a.m. and 5 p.m. is roughly 35 percent to 50 percent. At any given time more than one-half of workspaces are unused. (Trenck 2006)

This underutilization of workspace has led companies to develop solutions allowing for more efficient use of office space. These solutions allow companies to move workspace utilization from one person for each workspace to several people per workspace. It is common for firms to assign five or seven people per workspace on a shared or rotating basis. As a result, businesses and organizations can save millions in office space costs.

Examples include BearingPoint, which reported eliminating more than 4,000 workspaces nationwide resulting in more than $40 million per year in reduced real estate costs. Deloitte & Touche reported savings of nearly $132 million per year in real estate costs in the firm's New York and Chicago offices alone. And IBM reports saving nearly a half billion dollars over five years. (Trenck 2006)

CoreNet Global, a professional association for corporate real estate executives, conducted a study in 2004, *Corporate Real Estate 2010: Enabling Work in a Networked World (CoRE 2010)*. The study indicated that at least 25 percent of corporations' knowledge workers will work remotely by 2010, a prediction that gradually is coming true.

"Today's real estate professional is wearing three hats: real estate executive, IT strategist and human resources manager," according to Eric Bowles, director of global research for CoreNet Global.

The research also showed that the "demand for assigned or traditional office space will decrease substantially by 2010 as corporations rely on unassigned office space for workers." The survey found that these early projections and workplace practices are indeed infiltrating companies, and alternative workplace features are being found in respondents' existing workplaces:

- 73 percent of respondents said they introduced or increased desk sharing/unassigned workstations in the past year.
- 69 percent said improved ergonomics, lighting, comfort and functionality were deployed in the past year.
- 69 percent said introduced or increased drop-in spaces were deployed in the past year.

Survey findings also indicated that measurement processes and techniques and objective measurements were seen as a focus for commercial real estate leaders. "Many companies want to measure performance but need ways to measure effectively over a range of factors," Bowles said.

Survey respondents indicated that they measure total occupancy costs, and that most measure cost per workstation and cost per person housed. All respondents measure utilization and most measure meeting room use, workplace effectiveness and quality of environment, personal comfort and well being. (WorldatWork *Newsline* 2007)

Business Continuity

It's impossible to know when an interruption to operations will strike. From calamities like hurricanes or terrorist acts, to seemingly minor events like sudden ice storms, severed power lines or traffic tie-ups, the risk of sudden disruptions needs to be managed to mitigate the effects on an organization. That is the essence of business continuity (BC) planning—ensuring an organization has contingencies in place allowing it to operate and quickly recover from a disruption.

BC planning, which often focuses solely on corporate infrastructure, also needs to take into account the human factor: How can an organization's employees maintain productivity when faced with interruptions? The answer lies in the increased use of a mobile workforce.

To date, little knowledge has been available on how to develop and execute effective BC plans that incorporate telework. Slightly less than one-half of the organizations contacted by ITAC for its 2005 research report, *Exploring Telework as a Business Continuity Strategy*, included telework in their business continuity plans. Twenty-one percent indicated that telework was highly integrated with their BC plans, and 25 percent noted that telework and BC were lightly integrated. Forty-one percent of responding organizations were not integrated and 13 percent were unsure of their telework/BC plans.

An organization's ability to maintain normal operations during a major interruption can mean the difference between business success and failure. A wide variety of events can trigger a response. As the risk of disruptions increases and the magnitude of various events grow, the need to plan for those events increases as well.

BC planning, also called contingency of operations planning (COOP) by the U.S. government, allows organizations to proactively approach protecting the enterprise against threats to facilities, employees and other assets.

The effects of a disruption on business health are far-reaching. Revenue losses and diminished productivity lead the list of consequences. An unplanned closure can damage a company's reputation with customers, business partners, suppliers and shareholders.

Missing contract deadlines can leave an organization open to litigation. Insurance costs can skyrocket. Recovery costs associated with new facilities, replacement equipment, temporary workers or unplanned overtime can upset cash flow.

- One in five U.S. companies suffered a business interruption causing their organization to cease operations for a period of time, according to findings of a Partnership for Public Warning study commissioned by AT&T in 2004. (Opinion Research Company 2004)
- The cost of downtime from a disruption can quickly wipe out profits. Among *Fortune* 1000 companies, the average loss per hour of downtime is $78,000 and companies reported an average of 38 hours downtime per year, according to a study by market research firm Find/SVP. (Contingency Planning Research 2003)
- Forty-three percent of companies hit by severe crises never re-open their doors. The crises' ripple effect causes another 29 percent to fail within two years. (Cerullo 2004)
- The potential business impact resulting from a business interruption includes

reduced employee productivity (62 percent), reduction in profits (40 percent) and damage to customer relationships (38 percent). (Veritas 2004)

Traditionally, recovery has been concerned with protecting information systems, with little or no attention paid to the people who use those systems. Few plans addressed the possibility of loss of workplace access or, worse yet, loss of workers. Sadly, Sept. 11, 2001, was a wake-up call for continuity planners. It brought to light that continuity planning had to consider people issues. Increased threats of terrorism, infectious epidemics and workplace violence have forced organizations to re-evaluate business continuity plans and include human factors in their deliberations. These situations have led to the realization that telework is a viable tool for dispersing a company's most valuable asset: its people.

Remote work programs increase organizational flexibility and help companies rebound from crises more quickly. Telework helps organizations reduce recovery expenses and helps to boost competitive advantage. Best yet, through geographic dispersal of the workforce, it protects employees from potential harm. (ITAC 2005)

Chapter 8 will provide more detail on how to integrate telework into a company's business continuity plan.

Being a Good Citizen

Traffic congestion is a serious problem for most major metropolitan areas in the United States, particularly during the morning and evening commute hours. Not only do traffic tie-ups waste employees' time, this congestion also increases air pollution.

The Best Workplaces for Commuters reports the following on the effect commuting is having on the United States:

- 78 percent of all commute trips nationwide are drive-alone. (2000 Census)
- Between 2002 to 2012 drive-alone commuting vehicle miles traveled (VMT) will increase by at least 15 percent, generating an additional 43 million metric tons of carbon dioxide annually.
- The number of urban areas with more than 20 hours of annual delay per peak traveler has grown from five in 1982 to 51 in 2003.
- Approximately 2.3 billion gallons of gasoline are wasted to engines idling in traffic jams.
- Cost of congestion in 2005 is $63.1 billion per year. (Best Workplaces for Commuters 2006)

The removal of 175 cars from the road can save nearly 44,000 gallons of gasoline, and reduce global warming pollution (caused by carbon dioxide) by 460 tons every year.

In addition to reducing congestion and pollution, the type of commute required can affect new employee attraction. A 2005 GfK NOP survey found that a majority (85 percent) of commuters surveyed reported commute consideration as "important" in determining where they work or look for work, with the largest proportion reporting such considerations as "very important." Less than one in five (15 percent) deemed such commute considerations as "not at all important." (Best Workplaces for Commuters 2006) A company that demonstrates its commitment to improving the local environment increases its attractiveness to prospective employees.

For the employer to reap the full benefits of telework, HR needs to work closely with other departments including legal, facilities management, continuity of operations and IT on implementation. The following chapters lay out the details for the various departments in the successful implementation of telework.

Chapter 3

Developing the Telework Program

A successful telework project's specific design can vary according to the wide array of organizational applications and circumstances. One size does not fit all. But to get started, a generic prototype of project management design is presented. This provides a basis for more detailed discussion of recommended practices. All important design steps, recommended practices and additional references are presented in this chapter.

Before Getting Started

It is important to identify some key players in the process.

Program Manager

The program manager, often known as the "telework program coordinator," kicks off the project, tracks deliverables and keeps activities progressing. The program manager's first step is to become familiar with telework in general.

Telework program managers can come from one of several different departments including HR, IT or facilities management. The department of origin often is determined by the company's primary objective for implementing telework. If the purpose is to reduce office space cost, then facilities managers take the lead. If the goal is to improve employee attraction and retention, then HR likely will hold this leadership position.

Executive Champion

This individual is critical to the project's success and will support several arenas, interfacing with the leadership teams and offering guidance to overcome roadblocks between departments. The champion also ensures that adequate funding is secured for the program once the plan is accepted. The executive champion also may be the one who approves the position of a dedicated program manager. It is best if such a person is a C-level executive to provide the range of support needed.

The executive champion should be someone who understands the potential effect of telework as a business strategy that increases employee engagement and retention, along with reducing operational costs. The champion must be enthusiastic and strongly motivated by the compelling business reasons behind telework.

The Cross-Functional Project Team

Forming a cross-functional project team is fundamental to the success of a telework program. It is important to identify and involve the stakeholders who will be responsible for the program's planning, implementation and ongoing management. The program manager should recruit professional, motivated individuals from among the stakeholders. Participants should include individual business unit champions and staff from HR, IT, real estate and/or facilities, finance and/or procurement, training, legal/risk management and business continuity.

Prototype of Project Management

Telework project management can be broken into the following five phases. Each phase will be discussed in this chapter.

Program planning	1 to 9 months
Program funding	0 to 1 month
Program setup	1 to 6 months
Teleworker implementation	Ongoing
<u>Program management</u>	<u>Ongoing</u>
Total time to implementation	2 to 16 months

The time to deliver the program depends on the solution's complexity and whether it is developed and delivered in-house or outsourced. Timelines also depend on the availability of the key resources required for the cross-functional team. Program planning and program setup are sequential processes; therefore, the timeline cannot be condensed through parallel processing.

Keys to success include:
- Planning a solution that delivers measurable objectives
- Tracking information on project achievements to measure success
- Clearly defining processes of installation and support

- Using technology to provide teleworkers with the correct tools to do their jobs
- Expecting and budgeting for ongoing teleworker support.

Two more critical keys to success are an attention to detail and exercising due diligence.

Phase 1: Program Planning

Planning involves answering the questions necessary to understand and maximize telework's business impact on the organization and the employees. The ultimate challenge is to integrate telework seamlessly with an organization's core business so that telework eventually is regarded as an important management tool.

An issue that has been debated within the telework field is whether a business should have the flexibility to implement a formal or informal telework program. An *informal telework program* refers to a program in which managers are provided the flexibility to allow their employees to telework on an as-needed basis, (such as a doctor's appointment or staying home with a sick child). For an employer to realize the full benefits of telework, a *formal telework program* needs to be adopted involving key departments throughout the organization as outlined in the following pages of this chapter.

It is recommended that a program planning document be developed assessing the influence of telework on an organization. The document should be delivered in one to nine months, and includes:
- Telework objectives and measurements for how they will be achieved
- Telework solution and identification of who "owns" the telework program by function
- Business case analysis, complete with costs and savings
- Telework implementation timeline and plan.

The project team remains responsible for creating a telework strategy, developing policies, procedures and technical solutions supporting the telework program, and setting specific objectives. General objectives (e.g., reducing employee stress, improving the balance between work and family, or improving employee satisfaction and morale) are laudable, but specific objectives are better and provide something concrete and measurable. Objectives associated with telework might include:
- Reduce real estate expense (e.g., a 20-percent reduction within two years)
- Attract and retain quality workers (e.g., reduce labor turnover from 25 percent to 10 percent within 18 months)
- Increase employee productivity gains (e.g., by 15 percent within 18 months)
- Comply with regulations such as the Clean Air Act or local zoning regulations

(e.g., reducing citations 50 percent within 18 months)
- Reduce employee commuter trips (e.g., reducing VMTs by 20 percent within 18 months)
- Improve customer service levels (e.g., reducing complaint calls by 10 percent within one year)
- Strengthen good corporate citizenship (e.g., double the number of favorable media articles within one year).

Departments Represented in the Planning Process

Because telework affects most departments, a successful program requires the team effort of individuals representing key departments. Each department contributes its expertise, but coordination and information sharing among departments are essential to ensure a quality program. During the planning phase, the executive champion and cross-function executives should be updated regularly and invited to provide input.

The Cross-Functional Project Team

The cross-functional project team will develop the overall telework policy, soliciting input on such concerns as:
- Definitions of telework
- Public relations, internal and external
- Selection process and qualifying job functions for teleworking
- Selection of candidates to telework and qualifying attributes
- Management approval steps
- Responsibilities of employee and employer
- Teleworker agreement
- Hours of work
- Tax guidelines and implications
- Employee expenses (reimbursable and nonreimbursable)
- Use of employee vehicle
- Mail delivery
- Procedures for obtaining equipment, supplies and services
- Procedures for tracking maintenance and recovery of equipment, furniture and other assets
- Training requirements and schedule
- Systems to schedule and monitor implementation and work flows
- Continual policy re-enforcement

- Assurance of ongoing telework program value
- Change management.

The departments typically represented in the planning process are listed below and provide expertise in their specialized areas:

- Human Resources, with responsibilities including:
  - Selection and placement advice
  - Compensation and benefits administration advice
  - Development and delivery of telework-related training modules
  - Long-term program administration
  - Development of ROI metrics
- Legal, with responsibilities including:
  - Insurance burden clarification (corporate and employee)
  - Injury liability clarification (teleworker, family/friends, service engineers and customers)
  - Procedures for replacement/repair of damaged equipment
  - Theft prevention and incident reporting procedures
  - Protection of trade secrets and confidential files/data
  - Tax liability clarification (corporate burden reduction and general guidelines)
  - Procedures for reporting on-the-job accidents/injuries
- IT (voice, data and network), with responsibilities including:
  - Standards (network, desktop and support accessories)
  - Computer/network security
  - Computer equipment and security
  - Proposed configurations (levels of service)
  - Access to computer networks (LAN/CWAN)
  - Voice services (local exchange company) or voice-over Internet protocol (VoIP)
  - Installation support
  - Help desk support, especially beyond the traditional "normal" daytime work hours
  - Definition of any interdepartmental charges from internal IT for voice, data and network connections
  - "Hoteling" system and software to operate
- Procurement, with responsibilities including:
  - Provisioning process and billing requirements
  - Desktop equipment/accessories/supplies
  - Asset acquisition, tracking, servicing and reclamation
- Facilities management, with responsibilities including:
  - Space management (plans to accommodate growth, space relinquished by

teleworkers, billing process, any internal interdepartmental changes per square foot, etc.)

- Space definition and standardization (home office, hoteling/free address, telework center, etc.)
- Furniture policy development and enforcement (recommended setup, new furniture funding, surplus furniture, etc.)
- Ergonomics and safety (standards, applicability, home inspection policy, incident reporting procedures, etc.)

• Training department, with responsibilities including:
- Identify requirements, establish goals and develop and administer courseware for teleworkers, telemanagers and their respective co-workers
- Meet the training needs of all participants in understanding policies and procedures, expectations, reporting obligations, work conditions, setting up the office, communications, performance, managing distractions and termination of telework rights
- Satisfy the training needs of teleworkers in understanding a safe, successful work environment, social interaction, use of technology tools, security, professionalism, interaction with co-workers, management and customers, preventing overwork and isolation, handling dependent care, reporting work activities, record keeping and the terms of telework
- Meet the training needs of telemanagers in managing a remote workforce, setting objectives, measuring performance, maintaining work group communications and cohesion, reporting telework activity and preventing workload shifting

• Departments participating in the telework trial, with responsibilities including:
- Help set the telework program goals
- Provide feedback on the telework program and whether its goals are achieved

• Business continuity office, with responsibilities including:
- Identify goals for the remote-work continuity plan
- Investigate risk factors and identify how telework can help mitigate risks
- Identify resources needed for implementing telework as a BC strategy
- Compare costs for implementing telework versus the cost of housing essential employees in workplace-recovery centers
- Select the telework solution that best mitigates the risks the organization is most likely to face
- Formalize procedures for when and how employees should telework during expected emergencies

- Test and maintain readiness of the telework plan to ensure business continuity (don't wait until an emergency strikes to see if the plan works).

The Telework Plan

Once the team is in place and the program manager records its input, the next step is to develop the telework plan. At a minimum, the plan should include:

- Program objectives and how their achievement will be measured
- Definitions and policy details
- Business case, including startup and ongoing costs
- Technology plan
- Implementation plan.

The plan should document the program's projected effect on the organization, answer the questions given to the cross-functional managers and detail the business case and implementation plan. The implementation plan should begin at funding approval and end with an identified number of teleworkers being set up at home or other locations in a specific month.

To keep everyone heading in the same direction, hold cross-functional meetings every week. The program manager should keep an action list, track progress and encourage managers to network with others involved with telework programs.

Phase 2: Program Funding

A primary purpose of the program planning document is to make the case for project funding. Members of the team also should expect to make an executive summary presentation to the champion and others whose employees participated on the project team. This presentation should focus on the project history, the conclusions of the business case analysis, the top telework drivers relevant to the organization's objectives, rollout timelines, technology, competitive advantage and cultural effect on the organization.

After the information is presented, executives may ask for additional research and planning. If executive buy-in is high during the planning phase, the time needed to obtain funding is reduced. Once the planning phase is completed and budget dollars are allocated, program setup can begin.

Objectives

The time to obtain program funding ranges from one meeting to several months, depending on the size and complexity of the organization's operations. Approval may be granted at the first meeting, but do not be surprised if additional work is needed before final approval.

Keep the executive champion current on progress, objective by objective. When meeting for approval, focus on the financials and how progress relates to the tele-work plan and the organization's bottom line. Outside experts and case studies often add credibility.

Phase 3: Program Setup

The program setup involves all activities to move the project from the approval stage to installation of the first teleworker in his or her home office or other location(s). This can be a challenging time as outcomes will depend on the complexity of the technology, plan and measurements of progress. The program setup may include:

- Developing courses and scheduling classes for teleworkers and their managers
- Technology readiness of services, equipment, testing, etc.
- Demonstration area of suggested home office layout and setup
- Installation logistics (e.g., furniture, printer/fax, computer/communications technologies, ordering and installation)
- Contact information (who to call about what issues)
- Intranet to supply information for employees, managers and teleworkers
- Database to track information
- Surveys to provide feedback on the installation, support phases and employee satisfaction
- Reviews of the program to monitor achievement of objectives, identify lessons learned and modify plans based on experience.

Program setup is complete when the first teleworker is ready to begin. The time to delivery in this phase is from one to six months depending on the complexity of the plan, size of the organization, and whether tasks are done in-house or outsourced. A recommended practice is to use project management software to keep track of the activities. It also provides an easy way to summarize information when making periodic reports to the executive champion and other key decision makers.

Phase 4: Teleworker Implementation

The objective of this phase is to roll out the program. It is an ongoing process.

Telework Startup for Remote Workers

Actual startup can involve coordination of up to 40 events, some sequential, some parallel. Coordination is critical because the need to minimize any disruption to the teleworker and manager may affect the course of normal business and the program's success and credibility.

During startup, the rookie teleworker, having to operate outside the normal routine, may experience apprehension from the changes and possibly a decrease in productivity due to the newness of multiple office locations. It is common for the teleworker to experience highs (joys at not having to commute daily) and lows (missing an important document) in the first month. However, after a month, a productive routine often forms for the teleworker with his or her manager and colleagues.

Limit the first wave of teleworkers to 10 to 15 individuals, so any "bugs" in the process may be worked out and the process can be properly controlled.

Connectivity: A Key to Success

One word sums up the teleworker's ongoing needs: connectivity. The remote worker at home requires technical connectivity to the office and social connectivity to his or her co-workers, internal and external clients and manager. An organization's IT resources must be organized to support remote workers at home and on the road. Interpersonal connectivity can be encouraged and enhanced through teleworker events, rewards programs, focus groups, instant messaging, e-mail, conference calls, blogs, etc.

The program sponsors and executive champions, as well as skeptics of telework, also must remain connected by being kept informed of the program's results. As people learn more about telework, they will better understand how it complements the organizational business strategy. That, in turn, strengthens the program. This growth will be rewarding for the program manager, the program team, the champion, the teleworkers, the telemanagers and the entire organization.

Phase 5: Program Management

Once teleworkers are installed, the project shifts into the program management phase, which is managed by the telework coordinator.

The objectives of ongoing program management are:
- Track and deliver the business objectives of the program.
- Provide quality telework services, including speed, efficiency and feedback. Employ:
  - The best possible technical solution required
  - Effective installation processes and procedures
  - Ongoing help desk support for teleworker issues
  - Ongoing communication to the teleworkers and managers about significant successes or program changes.

- Generate high customer satisfaction responses for the telework support organization.
- Continually improve the cost model for support and technology: better, faster, cheaper!
- Provide ongoing measurements and measurable results.

This is an ongoing process. The objectives are delivered through:

- Establishing a plan to maintain control and integrity of the program
- Tracking teleworkers and their manager's satisfaction
- Tracking measurements and program progress through surveys and other feedback
- Marketing the program
- Monitoring and controlling setup costs and ongoing expenses
- Assuring and monitoring technical activities/problems
- Scheduling and monitoring delivery and installation
- Tracking and reporting reduced real estate expense
- Monitoring and avoiding employee relocation cost
- Monitoring and reducing new employee expense
- Monitoring and reducing costs of internal moves
- Monitoring effects on absenteeism and turnover
- Monitoring productivity changes
- Reporting program results
- Predicting and planning program growth.

ROI of Telework Programs

Telework can offer a variety of quantifiable benefits to employees and employers. Measuring the benefits of a pilot or ongoing program is critical to ensuring organizational support for telework as a standard operating procedure for employees whose jobs lend themselves to working from anywhere.

For HR, measuring the effect of telework on attraction and retention is critical to determining telework's value as a total rewards tactic. One way to measure these benefits is through metrics based on the four phases of the employee life cycle—attraction, joining, performing and leaving. Metrics measure telework's effect on the organization for each of these four phases. Details can be found in "Measuring Telework ROI: Metrics Based on the Employee Life Cycle" in Appendix B.

Experts recommended that practitioners provide quarterly status reports to the executive champion and business unit managers. Complete a yearly report outlining the achievement of business objectives by using the appropriate telework measurements as originally outlined during the business case analysis and funding justification.

Chapter 4

Successfully Managing
a Remote Workforce

Given the portability of computer and communications technologies, people can effectively work from almost anywhere at anytime. Thus, telework's implementation within an organization is becoming more complex simply due to the range of possible work locations and technologies. Entire departments, such as sales, are rarely in the employer's office and more likely to be on the road visiting clients or prospective clients than at "home." Other departments might have people working at home one day or two each week, while still others work at home less frequently to address occasional family concerns or maintain business continuity during business interruptions.

Most workers in midsize and large companies work on a regular basis with people they cannot see. In 2002, WFD Consulting found that working over a distance affects more than 80 percent of workers. (WFD Consulting Inc. 2002) Yet, for many senior managers "out of sight" can mean "out of mind." Put another way, managers continue to ask the question: "If I cannot see the people working for me, then how can I be assured they are getting the work done?"

Teleworker relationships with their managers, co-workers, subordinates and customers can become weakened without proper communication practices. Working remotely may increase the possibility of conflict between work and family roles; conflict among manager, co-worker and customer expectations regarding performance, and ambiguity about performance expectations. Working remotely also can inadvertently create the tendency to overwork simply because it is easy to work.

Role conflict, role ambiguity and work overload contribute to stress and can diminish work-life quality and the performance that telework is designed to provide. Remote workers must devote more attention to managing these aspects of their roles than their on-site co-workers do. An organization's HR management team can make an enormous difference between a successful initiative and a failed good idea in these areas. Like other important resources, such as funding and equipment, HR must be managed to ensure successful deployment.

Human resource management (HRM) refers to a comprehensive set of management practices ensuring the organization has a workforce that will allow it to achieve business goals and compete successfully. HRM practices are important when:

- Planning a new remote-work program
- Implementing such a program and
- Evaluating the program's success.

Planning Stage

HRM strategy should begin its focus by examining the reasons for encouraging remote work—to attract, retain and motivate/engage employees. In particular, HRM professionals must consider how remote work would strengthen the organization's human-resource system, such as the rationale in Figure 4-1.

Goals should be chosen carefully because they provide the outcomes that are measured when evaluating the program's effectiveness. This process should be done with a cross-functional team comprised of members high enough in the

Figure 4-1
HRM Strategic Goals for Remote Work

Attract New Employees	Enhance Performance and Retention	
	Motivate	Retain
• Recruit hard-to-find technical or other specialists • Provide opportunities for employees with disabilities	• Increase productivity • Enhance managerial skills • Enhance planning and organizing skills • Enhance innovation	• Retain essential employees and reduce turnover • Increase job satisfaction and morale • Increase organizational commitment and loyalty • Reduce absenteeism • Enhance work/nonwork performance • Provide scheduling flexibility

organization to have access to strategic information. A 2000 American Management Association (AMA) survey shows that 60 percent of remote-work programs that use cross-function teams rate their programs as highly successfully. Moreover, 89 percent of remote-work programs judged to be unsuccessful do not use cross-function teams. (AMA/ITAC 2000)

As a recommended practice, HR and telework experts believe that the HRM strategic plan should explain how teleworking supports the attraction, motivation and retention of employees, thus helping the organization gain a competitive advantage in a tight labor market.

Job Analysis/Competency Modeling

Job analysis, also referred to as competency modeling, is the practice of identifying the knowledge, skills, abilities and other factors required to perform the job successfully. This is essential for success in selection, training and performance appraisal. It also is important for protecting the organization from violation of laws concerning bias and discrimination in employment (e.g., the Civil Rights Act of 1964, the Americans with Disabilities Act).

Telework experts advise focusing on the specific job/position being considered for remote work and the relationship between the position and other positions in the organization. Also, remember to analyze the position and the work to be performed—not the potential teleworker.

Begin an analysis by focusing on these characteristics for the positions being considered for telework:

- How does the position get information that is required to perform the work (written materials, pictures and graphs), and what is the medium used (interpersonally, electronically)?
- Does the position require information processing, reasoning and problem solving, verbal and quantitative analysis?
- What are the working relationships with others (work alone or with others, deal with external customers, etc.)?
- How can the position's accomplishments be monitored and measured?
- What specific skills or expertise is required to do the position's work?
- Does the job allow the flexibility to work alone?
- Does the position require supervising others, giving direction, monitoring performance?
- Is communicating with others (sharing information, providing/seeking/accepting feedback) important?

- Is the work of the position portable?
- Does the position require specialized material or equipment that is only available at the office to effectively perform the work?

Recruiting Practices for Remote Work

Recruiting creates a pool of qualified applicants who may wish to work remotely. From the organization's perspective, workers are sought who possess the best skills and abilities. From the applicant's perspective, he or she will seek remote-work positions if they enhance personal or professional goals. The organization's goal in recruiting is to create an adequate pool of applicants to allow the organization to select the best candidates.

Use job analysis information describing knowledge, skills, abilities and other factors related to successful performance to write a job description for remote jobs. Requirements and expectations of the teleworker need to be described.

Selection Practices and Criteria for Telework Positions

Identify the best job candidates from the pool of applicants. Ideally, biographical information, tests, simulations, interviews, questionnaires and other reliable and valid measurements help to identify the best applicants—but the most reliable source will be historical reports on the person's work performance in the current position. Multiple selection methods and criteria should be used.

Selection for remote work can occur in two ways: reassign existing employees to remote work and/or hire external candidates. The selection criteria and methods to select external candidates should be more comprehensive than those used merely to reassign existing employees. Moreover, remote assignments may range from occasional telework to full-time "road warriors" who usually work away from the office. Selection criteria and methods for full-time remote work may be more comprehensive. The same job may have different requirements in different organizations. For example, some skills needed to be a successful desk clerk at a luxury hotel are different than those required of a desk clerk at a budget motel. Despite these differences, certain selection practices and criteria are likely to be common for most remote jobs.

What job experience is most helpful to become an effective teleworker? The following is important:

- Past successful experiences in telework
- Experience in working alone; demonstrated ability to solve problems without supervisory intervention

- Demonstrated ability to manage own time and work (i.e., being self-directed)
- Experience with needed hardware, software and other relevant equipment
- Strong record of performance.

What knowledge, skills and abilities are most-needed to be an effective teleworker? The following is important:

- Openness and adaptability to new experiences
- Internal motivation
- Self-discipline
- Conscientiousness
- Ability to function well without regular personal contact
- Ability to structure time, deadlines and work flow
- Ability to juggle multiple demands and complex projects
- Good organizational skills
- Goal-oriented
- Ability to recognize and analyze problems and apply any changes needed to complete tasks
- Good communication skills
- Initiative in seeking out and nurturing work relationships outside the workplace
- Appropriate home life (i.e., as freedom from distractions and demands)
- Availability of a separate area at home that is dedicated to work, free from distractions and meets safety requirements
- Physical abilities (i.e., ability to use computer keyboard or other data entry devices)
- Ability to work on-the-go from multiple locations.

Use structured interviews to ask candidates to describe how they would deal with situations involving conflict between work and family demands. Use work simulations to see how candidates deal with planning and organizing complex tasks on their own to meet a deadline.

Recommendations from supervisors, co-workers, subordinates and customers can be helpful in selecting strong performers. Before an existing employee becomes a teleworker, the manager should examine the impact of his or her absence on co-workers, customers and others.

Telework Agreement

In addition to the usual application questions and job description, a telework agreement with potential teleworkers should include a checklist of job criteria and a realistic job preview, such as:

- Minimal face-to-face contact will occur.

- Productivity will be monitored.
- Work-life conflict may arise.
- Regularly scheduled days/hours in the office may be expected so that others will know when he or she is available.
- A schedule for communicating and meeting with others is expected.

A telework agreement should also include a statement of equipment and communication needs and costs. It also should include a signature line for the employee, the line manager and the HR manager. To summarize:

- Use job analysis information to determine the remote job's requirements
- Use multiple criteria and selection practices to select strongest performers
- Use an application form that includes the relevant issues previously described
- Validate selection practices
- Use a written telework agreement.

Training for Remote Work

After selecting highly skilled and talented employees, training is required to prepare them to meet the unique demands of remote work in the organization. The AMA survey showed that two-thirds (66 percent) of remote-work programs judged to be highly successful provide training. Training should prepare remote workers, co-workers and supervisors to deal with the distance that separates them. For the remote worker, this means learning to plan and organize tasks without direct supervision. For co-workers, this means scheduling time for interaction and team activities. Supervisors must learn to lead, motivate and manage performance at a distance.

Training content must address relevant material and must be imparted successfully, using appropriate media and methods. Newly learned skills must be practiced and transferred to the job setting, where they should be rewarded and reinforced.

As a recommended practice from experts in the telework field: Conduct needs analyses and define training goals. Use needs analysis information to determine which individuals and organization units require training. Choose appropriate training content. Decide whether to outsource training. Evaluate effectiveness of training. Designing a training program for remote work consists of four steps:

- Identify the skills required to perform the job successfully and conduct a needs analysis.
- Create the training content.
- Deliver the training content to employees using appropriate methods.
- Determine effectiveness of the training.

Needs Analysis and Planning

Four points to consider are:

- Determine individual (employee and manager) need to acquire skills required for remote work.
- Determine organizationwide need for training.
- Gather information through interviews and questionnaires.
- Set goals for training based on needs analysis.
- Set goals for each individual with respect to need for training.
- Set goals for organization units with respect to need for training.

Training Content

Training content for participants includes:

- Communications skills
- Time management/planning and organizing skills
- Accepting responsibility/sense of ownership
- Setting up a home office and managing personal/family relationships while working from home (if applicable).

Training content for managers includes:

- Setting goals and managing by results
- Monitoring performance
- Giving feedback and coaching
- Remote motivation, leadership and performance management
- Setting expectations with teleworker and onsite co-workers.

The issue of training managers cannot be underestimated. Work-life expert Angie Laycock wrote:

> When new ways to manage people are expected, training on how to do this must be a priority. Simply raising expectations without changing the way supervisors communicate with their group will only defeat the goal of creating change. Training must include the understanding of stated policies and the provision of specific strategies for creating a flexible workplace while meeting business needs. (Laycock 2006)

Training content for remote workers includes:

- Time management/planning and organizing
- Setting goals and delivering results
- Dealing with possible work-life conflict and work interruptions

- Use of equipment
- Ergonomics and safety
- Legal concerns and requirements.

  Training content for co-workers includes:
- Effective time management to work in concert with teleworkers who may work different hours. (Core working hours are recommended to enhance communication among team members and enhance performance. Note that with some jobs, core hours may also be required to provide customer service.)
- Explaining to office-based employees that the remote colleague isn't "goofing off" or trying to shirk responsibilities.

Training Delivery

In the area of the delivery of the training:
- Choose an internal or an outsourced provider. The organization's HR or training staff provides internal training. Internal training is less expensive but staff may have little experience with remote work. Outsourced providers may be more expert and experienced but they cost more.
- Training methods should emphasize practice and transfer to the job.
- Distance learning is a strong option for some remote teleworkers.

Training Evaluation

In the area of evaluating the training:
- Assess reactions to training program: Did participants think they learned anything?
- Assess learning: Do participants know more about remote work after the training program than they did before the training program?
- Assess transfer to the job: Does an individual's performance improve as a result of the training?
- Assess the organizational unit: Does performance in the unit improve as a result of the training in remote work?

Implementation Stage

Performance appraisal is any system of determining how well an individual employee has preformed during a period of time, frequently used as a basis for determining merit increases. (WorldatWork 2007) Performance management uses information from the performance appraisal to monitor and manage performance. The AMA survey shows that nearly three-quarters (72 percent) of remote-work programs judged to be highly successful use performance appraisal methods to manage teleworkers.

Performance Appraisal and Management for Remote Work

In many respects, the appraisal and management of performance is no different for remote workers than for on-site workers. What is new is the movement of off-site workers who have traditionally worked on-site, such as data-entry clerks, administrative assistants and professional and technical workers.

An organization should develop a performance appraisal and management system that takes into account the physical separation of the employee and those who are responsible for monitoring and managing his or her performance.

Performance Appraisal

In the area of performance appraisal, the following tips apply:

- Establish job duties, expected accomplishments and expectations; explain how these relate to the organization, unit and work-group goals.
- Establish and communicate performance standards; emphasize measurable accomplishments and deliverables; be careful not to rely on on-site staff more because they are easily available.
- Have the individual evaluate the degree to which the goals and accomplishments were met.
- Determine who will assess performance: manager, self, co-workers, subordinates, customers or—in a 360-degree feedback system—everyone.
- Establish times for face-to-face contact.
- Establish methods for communication for various types of information and determine when to use e-mail, telephone, fax or face-to-face meetings.
- Observe performance when possible; when performance itself is not visible, observe outcomes of performance.
- Document incidents of good, average or poor performance.
- Recognize any performance constraints, such as the absence of needed information or resources, inadequate computer equipment in the home, conflicting demands and so forth.
- Taking organizational constraints into consideration, rate performance based on documented incidents.
- Share performance ratings with employee in writing and in a face-to-face meeting.

Performance Management

For performance management to work effectively, it is critical that the following four questions are addressed:

- Does the employee know what to do?
- Does the employee know how to do it?
- Does the employee want to do it?
- Is the employee allowed to do it?

To answer these questions, the following steps must be taken:

- Provide performance feedback, coaching, counseling and resources as needed.
- Provide opportunities to present successes of remote work throughout the organization.
- If performance improves, recognize and reward performance and encourage further development.
- If performance does not improve, implement a performance improvement plan and additional training.
- If unsatisfactory performance continues, transfer the employee to a nonteleworking job or begin termination process.
- Cycle through the performance appraisal and management process again.
- Provide a mechanism for appeal of the performance rating if employees feel that their ratings are unfair.

Compensation, Rewards and Benefits

Remote work is another method for doing the work others within the organization are doing. Remote workers should enjoy the same (or close to the same) compensation, rewards and benefits that on-site workers do. A concern, however, is the possibility of nonexempt remote employees working overtime without compensation, a violation of the Fair Labor Standards Act (FLSA). Nonexempt employees working remotely must account for their time and perform overtime only with advance approval. (See Chapter 7 for details.)

Managing Roles and Relationships in Remote Work

Relationships with one's manager, co-workers, customers and family are most affected by remote work. To keep the roles clear and the relationships strong, communication should be paramount. A few tips follow.

The manager should:

- Clarify expectations continuously—orally and in writing.

- Establish regular communication and reporting periods, such as weekly summaries of activities.
- Make certain the remote worker gets copied on memos and e-mails that are distributed in the unit.
- Set up a "buddy system" to keep remote workers informed of daily office news, memos and other relevant issues.
- Periodically examine the communication process to determine whether it is sufficient or requires change.

The teleworker should:
- Request a weekly team teleconference with manager and co-workers.
- Suggest meeting in person with manager or co-workers whenever possible.
- Make personal contact a priority when in the office.
- Establish times when others may call at home.
- Attend office parties and other scheduled social functions, such as going-away parties, baby showers and softball games.
- Have lunch with a colleague at least once every two weeks if teleworker's remote-work location permits.

The teleworkers also needs to let his or her colleagues know if they are feeling isolated. Those colleagues may make an effort to contact the telework on a more frequent basis. Teleworkers should also develop an "office frame of mind" at home by:
- Creating a quiet environment that is isolated from family traffic.
- Waking up at the same time each day.
- Establishing a ritual that marks the beginning of work every day, such as reading e-mail.
- Setting up and following a work schedule.
- Letting unfinished personal projects wait for a break in the work schedule.
- Making a "To Do" list at the end of each day and using it to keep focused on the next day's work.
- Establishing breaks as appropriate.
- Dressing (although informally) for work.

To enhance work-life balance, the teleworker should also consider the following:
- Avoid overwork by establishing a work schedule and "nonwork" hours. Resist nonwork activities during scheduled work time.
- Explain to family members that working at home is not a substitute for child care or elder care. Set ground rules for acceptable interruption and by controlling unannounced interruptions, such as for pre-agreed situations when family members become ill.

- Give family members "permission" to complain when work at home disrupts family activities.
- Take advantage of company-sponsored programs for work-life balance.

Evaluation

Planning is by far the most important phase of evaluation. During this stage, identify stakeholders, determine an appropriate match between data collection methodology and type of data needed, identify projected communications and establish timing and milestones.

Planning Evaluation

Evaluation has two emphases: outcomes and processes. Outcome evaluation shows whether the program was successful. Process evaluation shows why the program was successful.

Outcome evaluation focuses on the result of the intervention or change. Outcome evaluation should include examining goals for the remote-work program, such as the extent to which it increases productivity and job satisfaction through improved retention rates. Process evaluation focuses on how the outcomes were achieved, such as whether job satisfaction increased because remote work provided flexible scheduling, which, in turn, resulted in enhanced work-life balance.

Data Collection

Evaluation focuses on the measurement of change in important indicators of success. For remote work, these indicators might include increases in job satisfaction and productivity, reductions in absenteeism and turnover and so forth.

Some form of measurement must be used to assess change in these indicators. Ways to measure include questionnaires, interviews, behavioral observations and ratings, or company data, such as sales records. The quality of measurement is important. If measures are not reliable and valid, they yield data that may lead to inappropriate conclusions concerning telework's effectiveness. Organizations that do not have internal research staff with experience in psychological and organizational measurement should outsource this activity.

The program's measurement goals and the number of individuals who must supply information drive the development of the data-collection process. In a small telework pilot, conducting face-to-face or phone interviews may be most appropriate to gather information. If, however, a large-scale telework program is in place, a questionnaire may be the preferred mode of data collection.

Interpretation and Use of Data

After data are collected, they must be analyzed and interpreted. This involves the use of statistics to determine whether the changes that are observed are due to telework or to chance. It also is possible that desired outcomes, such as job satisfaction, decline rather than increase. Statistical analysis allows one to draw the proper conclusions regarding the telework's effectiveness. Organizations that do not have internal research staff should outsource this activity.

Action Planning

Actions resulting from an evaluation are based on the nature of the evaluation results. If the results suggest that things are going well, then no change is needed. Otherwise, the remediation/to-do list will come directly from the evaluation results.

Program Evaluation in Remote Work

An evaluation of a telework should include the following points:

- Identify HRM outcomes/goals that are expected to result from the remote-work program.
- Identify processes likely to lead to outcomes identified in previous step (e.g., reduced commuting time and enhanced work-life balance will increase job satisfaction).
- Determine how to measure all outcomes and processes and create or purchase required measurement instruments; ensure reliability and validity of all measures.
- Choose an evaluation design to determine causal influence of telework. Examples:
  - Measure the remote-work group before and after training and assignment to remote work. Compare change in scores on all measurements after employees have been working remotely for a sufficient time, such as six to 12 months. An increase in scores may be attributed to the remote-work program.
  - Measure two similar groups: one group that received the training and was assigned to remote work, and another group that does not receive the training and remained on-site. Compare differences in scores on all measurements before the remote-work assignment and after working remotely for a time. Also, compare change in the scores between the two groups over time.
- Use evaluation results to revise the remote-work program as needed.
- Use evaluation results to plan dissemination of the program throughout the organization.
- Repeat evaluation process as necessary.

As mentioned in Chapter 3, organizations can evaluate the effectiveness of a program by applying metrics to the Employee Life Cycle. Through such metrics, a company can compare teleworkers with nonteleworkers. An excellent example of how such metrics are applied was described in Chapter 1 with Aetna insurance—a company that compared retention rates between their teleworkers and nonteleworkers.

Telework experts note as a recommended practice that work objectives for teleworkers be kept concrete and measurable and the standards for success be communicated. Tie the evaluation of telework to the HR strategic plan. Identify expected outcomes and processes. Use reliable and valid measures of all outcomes and processes. Choose an evaluation design that allows the clearest judgment of the program's effectiveness. Use statistics to analyze the results. Use evaluation results to develop an action plan to guide telework and organizational change.

Chapter 5

Technology Is Critical for Virtual Worker Productivity

Advances in computer and communications technology have, in large part, made possible cost-effective, productive remote work. Powerful personal computers, mobile phones, e-mail and high-speed Internet connectivity are essential to the smooth running of a distributed work program. This chapter examines some issues involved in assessing technology to support remote work that supports the organization's business continuity (BC) strategy.

Issues to Consider

The technology to support teleworkers during an event interrupting business operations is similar to the technology used by everyday teleworkers, but some issues become magnified during an emergency. Connectivity and security, for example, become more critical as more employees may need remote access to the corporate network.

Certain crucial issues need to be kept in mind when establishing a BC/telework technology program.

Scope

When considering technology solutions, organizations should first identify the scope and type of BC solution they plan to implement. For example, in planning a skeleton BC solution, when only a small portion of the workforce will be used during an emergency, the technology needs will be relatively simple. If, on the other hand, the company needs a large portion of the workforce back in business, the issues become more complex.

Mobility

The ability to disperse equipment along with staff is a powerful incentive to include mobility in the equipment-buying decision. Laptop computers equipped with wireless connectivity, cell phones and devices such as the BlackBerry encourage the anywhere/anytime connectivity that can ensure productivity and active communications from suddenly scattered employees.

Productivity

A standard technology platform—as opposed to, for example, an informal mix of home computers with different software and standards—can help ensure that workers remain productive. In reviewing technology policies, consider issues influencing a remote employee's ability to get his or her job done—issues like training, help desk support and the speed at which files can be accessed. Be on the lookout for ancillary tasks that take more time or effort when done remotely. For example, how efficient is the remote network access? Do employees waste time trying to dial in to the network? Would it be less frustrating for employees to use a virtual private network (VPN) connection?

Scalability

If a large-scale emergency event occurs, there may be a need to ramp up a remote work program quickly. Can the technology infrastructure support a potential upsurge in usage? For example, many remote users will require additional network capacity and tech support. New hardware and software also must be procured quickly. Plus, these assets need to be tracked and managed.

Connectivity

The ability to connect to a corporate network and stay in touch with displaced team members is critical to any BC strategy. Review technology decisions with connectivity in mind. How will remote workers access files and other critical information? What tools will be needed to ensure effective, ongoing collaboration? How will voice communications be managed?

Redundancy

BC requires comprehensive backup strategies to limit the effect of failures of internal and external equipment and services. Look at discovering multiple ways that users will connect to the network, consider how telecommunications services are provisioned, review data backup strategies, and negotiate terms-of-service agreements with providers governing network backup and uptime guarantees.

Cost

If an organization plans on resituating many employees, many of whom may not be equipped with remote access and/or remote facilities, consider contracting for emergency technology. This may be more cost effective than maintaining access that will be used only in an emergency. Providers are beginning to develop such on-demand contracting options. Federal agencies, for example, have access to franchises and cooperative administrative support units that provide cooperative contracting options on a wide range of technologies.

Another option is using surplus (previous-version) hardware to support mobile users. Instead of simply getting rid of it, much of this hardware can still be used for basic alternate worksite work, and it is still standard.

Security

Dispersed workers bring new challenges in terms of data and network security. An increased amount of sensitive, proprietary information will be accessed by and reside with remote workers. Public networks, such as the Internet, are used as a way into a private corporate network. New types of gear may also bring new security risks. Consider physical security (how, for instance, to keep laptop computers from being stolen) and data security. Look at security inside a company as well as security measures that need to be employed where a remote worker is stationed. In the following pages, specific mention is made of the security issues related to each area of the technology discussed.

For many organizations, security is the top challenge facing IT managers, even ahead of cost control and containment. According to IDC's 2004 Enterprise Technology Trends survey, spending on security and business continuity worldwide is expected to grow twice as fast as IT spending during the next several years, surpassing $116 billion by the end of 2007. (IDC 2004) Employer security policies are outlined in Figure 5-1 on page 44.

Computers and Other Equipment

Teleworkers use a variety of tools to get work done. Computers are the most common. This section concentrates primarily on laptops and personal digital assistants (PDAs).

Figure 5-1
Employer Security Policies

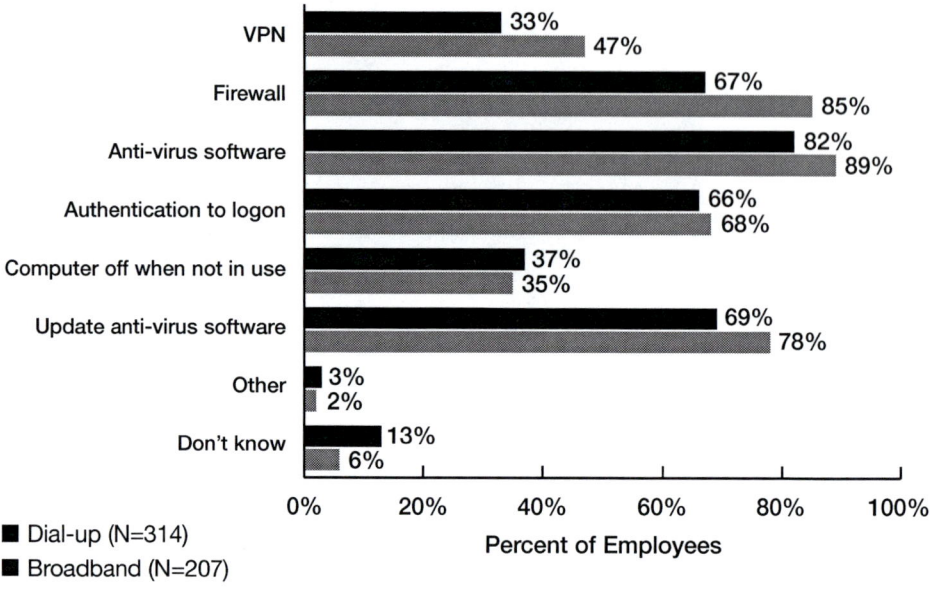

Dial-up (N=314)
Broadband (N=207)

Source: ITAC report, *"Teleworking Comes of Age with Broadband,"* Telework America Survey. 2002.

Laptop Computers

The issue for many companies is whether to equip remote workers with a laptop or desktop computer. For the past several years, the price/performance gap between laptops and desktops narrowed considerably, and it is now possible to get a business-grade laptop for under $1,000 from major computer manufacturers. Of course, it may not have the "bells and whistles" of the top-of-the-line laptop models, but it can easily handle normal computing needs. As a result, laptop sales are soaring. In the United States, laptop sales account for roughly 24 percent of all computer sales, according to Gartner research. (ZDNet 2006)

Desktop computers are still considerably less expensive than laptops, but buyers should not consider price alone when shopping for computing devices. Total cost of ownership (TCO) may be a more accurate gauge, especially when considered along with issues of overall productivity. TCO analyzes factors including initial hardware costs, maintenance contracts, cost of spare parts, IT training and staffing costs, network and telecommunications overhead, help desk support expenses and the cost of downtime.

Gartner's analysis indicates that a standard desktop computer costs an organization about $6,200 per year, while a laptop computer costs about $8,500 per year.

But the extra $2,300 cost of ownership for a laptop can be paid off with the higher productivity that mobile workers exhibit. In fact, employees outfitted with a laptop PC get up to three hours of increased productivity per week versus their deskbound counterparts. (Gartner Inc. 2001)

Portability

Laptops may not be the answer for an organization. Many employees dislike carting a laptop back and forth, especially a heavy one. Plus it's not always convenient to carry it on a subway, bus or train, or in inclement weather. Some organizations have found it more sensible to provide a desktop computer at the main office and equip remote workers with portable drives that they can pop into their pockets to conveniently take their files with them.

Consider the User

Gartner studies reveal that laptops used by traveling workers (those who are out of the office more often than day extenders) have a 25-percent higher TCO. (Troni and Fiering 2003) The higher TCO is caused by the additional demands that a mobile worker places on a laptop, increasing the possibility of damage. Unlike desktops, which have some standardized components, laptops are an assemblage of specialized parts. Day extenders and telecommuters, on the other hand, generally travel only between home and office, placing less stress on their equipment and reducing the possibility of loss or theft. As a result, their TCO is lower. Gartner estimates that it is only about 20-percent higher than that of a desktop model.

Create a policy for company-provided technology based on type of teleworker similar to the chart in Figure 5-2 on page 46. This standardizes the equipment the help desk must support and simplifies procurement decisions. Hewlett-Packard established an equipment policy with a matrix of the tool set available for teleworkers. It includes a headset, all-in-one printer, conference number or calling card.

Mobility Expense Reimbursement Matrix

Create standard mobile work packages. Some companies offer a menu of mobility tools; others specify toolsets based on the level of mobility. Figure 5-2 presents a sample.

Laptop Security Risks

By their nature, portable computers are riskier. It's easy for a thief to lift a laptop from a crowded airport, hotel lobby or the trunk of a car. The laptop may also contain sensitive information, confidential corporate data or passwords. According

Figure 5-2
Mobility Expense Reimbursement

	Traditional Office	Traditional Non-Office	Customer Location	Mobile/ Teleworker	Traveler/ Transition	Home- Based
Home office telephone line						•
Home office telephone purchase						•
Broadband data line						
Long distance business calls	•	•	•	•	•	•
Long distance conference call service	•	•	•	•	•	
Cell phone service	•	•	•	•	•	
Handheld wireless e-mail device			•	•	•	
Wireless PC data card				•	•	
Printer/all-in-one machine						•
Office furniture allowance						•

Definitions:
Traditional office—Employee has dedicated office space in a company-provided building.
Traditional non-office—Employee is housed in a company-provided building but has no dedicated office space.
Customer location—Employee works at customer office.
Mobile/teleworker—Employee has no dedicated office space and uses a number of workspaces.
Traveler/transition—Employee is a frequent traveler or is transitioning to a more mobile work style.
Home-based—Employee has a dedicated home office and no office in company-provided building.

Source: ITAC Telework/BC Research, 2004

to the U.S. Federal Bureau of Investigation, only 3 percent of stolen computers are recovered. (Burnell 2002) In 2001, 39 laptops were stolen for every desktop PC that was pilfered, according to a report by Safeware, a computer insurance company. (Safeware Insurance Group 2001)

During the three-year period from 2000 to 2003, an estimated 1.6 million PCs were stolen in the United States. A 2003 joint study by the Computer Security Institute and the FBI estimated that the average cost to a company per mobile PC stolen is more than $47,000 per incident reported. (Federal Bureau of Investigation 2003) And yet, according to Gartner, 73 percent of companies do not have specific security policies for mobile devices. (Sinrod 2003) Some tips for preventing laptop theft are presented in Figure 5-3.

Use of Personal Equipment

The majority of American knowledge workers have a home PC and Internet access. These employees can become emergency teleworkers in a crisis. If organizations decide to take advantage of these "accidental teleworkers," what issues arise?

Experts say that hidden costs exist to supporting home teleworkers using their own equipment because IT staffs must support and troubleshoot multiple applications. According to Cisco's Stephen DuMont, this can result in shadow IT projects, special configurations and a significant drain on limited resources. (DuMont 2004)

If teleworkers share the home network with other family members, for example, networks can be exposed to viruses and worms that teleworkers could unwittingly transmit to the enterprise network when they log in.

"One of the most costly mistakes is to support a user's own equipment rather than having an IT department do the purchasing," said Phillip Redman, Gartner's research vice president in an interview with Mobile Computing magazine. "Prices are higher and individual devices are harder to support. If the IT department purchases the devices, they will get a better price and can employ tools to help with management. Returns and repairs will also be easier to manage." (Rendon 2004)

At the least, develop a telework policy explaining what applications and hardware the IT staff will support. Include a statement allowing IT staff to access their home computers remotely and download virus protection software. Require a personal firewall.

Figure 5-3
Tips for Preventing Laptop Theft

- Don't leave computer in plain sight in a vehicle, locked or not. Cover it or place it in the trunk of your car.

- Equip the laptop with a two-way wireless security alarm. If the alarm detects movement, it can trigger the machine to start wailing at 110 decibels.

- To foil thieves, experts suggest carrying laptops in a briefcase or other carrying case not specifically designed for laptop use.

- Lock it or lose it. When in an office environment, use a cable lock that wraps around an immovable object to anchor your laptop until your return.

Handheld Devices

Increasingly, road warriors are moving their work to PDAs, which are useful for taking quick notes, getting and sending e-mail, and keeping calendar and contact information up-to-date. And, because these devices are so small, they have a higher chance of being carried out of a building in an office evacuation. When the discovery of the deadly toxin, ricin, closed the Hart Senate Office Building, staffers continued to work from other offices, home and even Capitol Hill coffee shops.

"Due to technology, we've all been in constant contact, through BlackBerry handhelds, cell phones and laptops," said Kristin Pugh, spokesperson for Senator Lisa Murkowksi, in an interview with reporters at the *Anchorage Daily News*. (Ruskin 2004)

Not all teleworkers need a laptop. Many only need a method to send and receive e-mail. It may be much less expensive to equip teleworkers with handheld e-mail devices or smart phones than a laptop computer. Gartner's analysis reveals that the two-year total cost of ownership for a PDA is $1,946 in 2004. (Rendon 2004)

PDAs with communications capabilities are useful tools in an emergency. In the hours and days after Sept 11, 2001, many telephone networks were down; others were overloaded. It was difficult, if not impossible, to place a telephone call in some areas. Though cell-phone networks and telephones were down, the BlackBerry network continued to work.

To recap, Figure 5-4 compares equipment type and the annual total cost of ownership as it existed in 2004.

Risky PDA Behavior

According to findings from the "Mobile Vulnerability Survey of 2004," commissioned by Pointsec Mobile Technologies, two-thirds of users store company information and client contacts on their PDAs. Almost one-half report that their equipment is e-mail enabled and one-third have telephone capability built in.

Yet, in spite of important business information residing on these machines, two-thirds of the PDA population uses no encryption to protect data and one-third don't password protect. Research also showed that 13 percent of users have lost their devices. (Pointsec Mobile Technologies 2004)

The best steps to take include the creating of a mobile security policy requiring users to assign passwords (and change them monthly), set their devices to lock down periodically, hide sensitive information, and learn how to encrypt data on their devices. Back up files daily onto a Universal Serial Bus (USB) drive or portable storage card and carry those files separately.

Figure 5-4
**A Comparison of Equipment Type and
the Annual Total Cost of Ownership (in 2004)**

Equipment Type	Annual TCO
Desktop computer	$6,200
Laptop computer	$8,500
Personal digital assistant (PDA)	$973

Source: Gartner

Collaboration Tools

Today, a majority of large public and private organizations share data and information and manage projects and employees from multiple locations and across time zones. They may e-mail documents or use collaborative applications such as groupware and instant messaging.

Productivity Software

Teleworkers require the same productivity software used by office workers, including word processing, spreadsheet and presentation applications. Be sure teleworkers have the same versions of these applications as other employees to ensure files and formatting can be shared across dispersed workgroups.

When routing documents, encourage users to take advantage of collaboration tools that are part of most productivity software packages. Microsoft Office, for example, includes features allowing users to track revisions and share documents in real time.

Groupware

As projects get more complex and users more widespread, many organizations turn to groupware solutions to allow employees to manage workflow, share files and calendars, and build a collaborative knowledge base. Groupware can include interactive conferencing tools such as discussion forums, chat rooms and electronic whiteboards, along with standard tools such as e-mail.

Instant Messaging

Instant messaging (IM), a popular application with home users, can also have a place in a business environment. Unlike e-mail, IM delivers messages directly to the desktop, demanding immediate attention. This can be a major asset or a major distraction. IM enables employees to communicate with colleagues, customers and partners in real time, like a telephone call, but without long-distance charges.

It's also useful for dual communications, such as getting information from a co-worker while on the telephone with a customer without having to put the customer on hold. Companies use IM or a variety of activities including staff meetings, immediate file transfer, remote brainstorming, customer service chat, training feedback and instant collaboration among e-workers. IM is helpful during emergencies because the Internet remains functional, even if local telephone services are down.

A 2004 study of IM users by the Pew Internet & American Life Project revealed that 11 million people use IM at work. (Pew Internet and American Life Project 2004) Gartner predicts that by 2006, IM will be used more frequently than e-mail as the preferred method of enterprise messaging.

IM Security Risks

Consumer IM programs were not designed for the enterprise and, therefore, lack security measures to protect company information. There is no user authentication, encryption, auditing or archiving. To access IM, companies must open some Web ports, which can put sensitive information and private data at risk. Another hazard in the instant messaging world is a new kind of unwanted commercial message, known as "spim." Ferris Research estimated that about 4 billion spam messages were sent in 2004, clogging company networks with yet another version of electronic junk mail. (Regan 2004)

If an organization decides to use IM, either as a backup communications service during emergencies or as a standard collaborative tool, it's important to set limitations. Make certain that user settings refuse file transfers from unknown persons. Restrict "buddy" lists (people who are welcome to chat) to legitimate business contacts only. Never use IM for confidential communications unless the IM system supports message encryption.

Some important steps to take include:
- Implement an enterprise-level IM program specifically designed to operate behind a firewall
- Install IM-management software to control user access, whether file transfer is allowed, and to filter or block content. These programs also allow administrators to monitor and review IM conversations. Monitoring becomes a necessity if an industry is regulated and a company needs to record all communications.

Real-World Experience

CARE, the worldwide humanitarian relief agency, uses Groove groupware to link relief workers in Central America with its IT staffers. The program allows remote workers to do their jobs even if an online connection isn't available. According to Richard Prather, CIO and vice president of technology, employees can work offline and then sync up automatically with other group members when they are able to get connected.

"That is a big benefit in remote locations where online connections and even electricity can be frequently cut off," Prather said in a July 2004 *Computerworld* article. (Weiss 2004)

IT staff at Alaska Airlines used Centrinity FirstClass collaboration tools to coordinate crises when flights were grounded for several days during the security lockdown that followed the attacks of Sept. 11, 2001. To keep employees, customers and other airlines informed of its plans, the airline quickly built online workspaces where the security team shared information and distributed security bulletins. (Maselli 2001)

Telephone Communications

In severe emergencies, a telephone is a lifeline—sometimes serving as the only link to the outside world. Preparation and planning can help employees stay connected when trouble strikes. Some communications alternatives that can help dispersed employees stay in touch with office and home follow.

Land-Based Telephone Service

The telephone network is tough. Telephone calls are routed through central offices that are built to withstand high winds, severe earthquakes and other weather-related catastrophes. But they cannot withstand "direct hits," as organizations learned during the World Trade Center attacks.

Even companies whose headquarters were not damaged on Sept. 11, 2001, had significant problems with telecommunications. When a Verizon communications hub was severely damaged, it affected telephone services throughout the region. More than 300,000 voice lines and 3.5 million data circuits in lower Manhattan were knocked out. (American Broadcasting Companies Inc. 2002)

During emergencies, local telephone circuits become overloaded because so many people try to make telephone calls simultaneously. Also, telephone instruments may get knocked off their bases, creating an open circuit. To help restore telephone service, instruct employees to check that telephones are back in their cradles.

Require that all home-based employees keep at least one telephone that does not need electricity to operate. Cordless phones and telephone systems are out of service if the electricity is out.

Call Forwarding

Handling office telephone calls can be a problem during an emergency. Organizations struggle to find ways to get customer calls through to the desired party when offices are closed for emergency events. For example, unless the organization plans to forward calls, calls may go unanswered. Some methods to forward calls include:

- Voice redirect. Prescripted service that sends a call to an alternate location. There is no flexibility, however, and the scripting must be done in advance of the emergency.
- Remote call forwarding. This service allows an individual user to specify where the call should be forwarded. The user does not have to be in the office to initiate call forwarding but can call from any phone. This method is less secure because a skilled phone hacker (or "phreaker") could commit toll fraud. It also requires that company infrastructure is still running.
- Internet-based phone extend tool. Using a Web browser, employees can redirect calls when needed and send the call to up to three different telephone numbers where the call will ring simultaneously. This lets the employee send calls to his or her cell phone, business line at home or alternate office.

Mobile Phones

Mobile phones are de facto emergency communications tools. Lightweight and low-cost, they are a remote worker's frequent companion. As of September 2006, there were more than 219 million wireless subscribers in the United States representing more than 72 percent of the total U.S. population, according to CTIA-The Wireless Association, an association for the wireless telecommunications industry. (Cellular Telecommunications & Internet Association 2006) Many employees have a personal cell phone, so be certain to capture that telephone number in an employee database for emergencies. And remember that mobile phones frequently fail in regional disasters, so include that consideration in plans.

Cell networks often stay operational even if landlines go down and can provide a good backup strategy. They are especially useful when power is out. However, cell networks were not built to support extremely high traffic so they too can suffer from congestion problems.

Text Messaging

During the Northeast Blackout of 2003, which affected the United States and Canada, most telephone networks kept working. However, because millions of people with cell phones were trying to make calls at the same time, operational systems were overloaded. One wireless technology continued to stay operational—short message service (SMS). SMS transmits tiny text messages to and from a mobile phone. Voice calls using the cell network require a lot of bandwidth whereas text messages can squeeze into small spaces on the network and transmit when they find a brief opening in the data flow. This makes SMS a highly reliable communications service.

In the aftermath of the Nigata earthquake in Japan in October 2004, the Ministry of Internal Affairs and Communications set up a cellular-phone message-board service using SMS. Citizens could leave messages and check messages from friends and family, using their DoCoMo cell phones. The user could report his or her status, such as "OK" or "in a shelter," and also leave a text message of up to 100 characters. (The Daily Yomiuri 2004)

A Roll of Quarters

Pay phones often operate sooner than normal home or business phones during an emergency. That's because they are part of the emergency service network and have a higher priority in the service restoration schedule. Make a note of pay telephones near the office building and include their location in a BC plan. Keep a roll of quarters or a spare phone card in the petty cash drawer or tape a few quarters on the back of an index card containing emergency information and telephone numbers.

Voice-over IP

Voice-over Internet protocol (VoIP)—or IP telephony—makes a phone conversation possible through the Internet or a dedicated IP network instead of using standard voice transmission lines. By using the Internet, VoIP can share existing bandwidth, making VoIP calls much lower in cost than traditional long-distance calls. And because the call setup is completely digital, rerouting calls to another location is easy.

Seventy-nine percent of executives surveyed plan to provide teleworkers with VoIP by 2006, according to a 2004 joint study by AT&T and the Economist Intelligence Unit. (AT&T 2004) One reason: cost savings. Companies can save more than 60 percent of their voice communications costs by switching from traditional circuit-based services to VoIP technology that uses a company's existing data network to route internal calls.

With VoIP, organizations no longer need expensive off-premises switches, separate voice lines to employee homes and long-distance charges. Calls within a VoIP network bypass local telephone companies. Instead, they are routed at low or no cost through a company's data network. VoIP is especially cost-effective when used in a mobile environment. Provided with VoIP via their laptop computers, workers can access their company network as well as calling features including voice mail, all through their broadband or wireless connection.

VoIP includes a "talking e-mail" feature allowing users to listen to voice mail over an Internet connection and forward it, as an e-mail, to others. This can be a valuable feature during an emergency when it may be necessary to communicate quickly with many employees.

Security is a concern whenever voice or information is routed through a public network, so if a company's organization decides to implement a VoIP phone solution, that company needs to be certain to implement security measures such as call encryption, user authentication and service authorization.

Cisco Systems was trialing an enterprise teleworker program when an ice storm disabled electrical power to several buildings at their North Carolina campus. With power out for several days, employees took their work home. Each teleworker trial team member had a VoIP phone at home. Neil Anderson, a manager in enterprise systems engineering at Cisco and member of the trial group, reported, "Using the IP phone was exactly like working at my desk. Colleagues and customers reached me on the same number and I received my voice mail in the same way. I had access to the full suite of business applications just as though I was sitting on Cisco's campus network."

Conference Calling

Bridge numbers used for remote teams are old standbys, but they become even more critical during emergencies. Randall Till, vice president of global business continuity management at MasterCard, establishes a 24-hour bridge number during emergencies.

"We conduct global meetings via teleconference and have upwards of 100 employees on a bridge call for discussion and management direction during an emergency situation," he said.

Diversify

Most regional disasters include telecommunications failures. Don't rely on only one communication solution. Instead, diversify communications choices. Use a mix of pagers, PDAs, cell phones and landlines. Work with a number of vendors and solutions. During the crisis that began on Sept. 11, 2001, cell phone service was down in some areas, landlines in others. The New York Mercantile Exchange issued essential employees cell phones enhanced with two-way radio capability. Employees also carry portable two-way e-mail devices—some with phone capability—and laptop computers with cellular modem cards that allow them to connect wirelessly to their office network anywhere cellular coverage is available. (Verton 2004) ITAC researchers found that organizations provided a variety of equipment and services to their teleworking employees. (See Figure 5-5)

Access

Remote workers need a way to connect to the office to send and receive e-mail, secure documents and software applications, and collaborate with colleagues. This section discusses Internet and network access.

Internet Access

Teleworkers likely will require Internet access, but the question is, at what speed should they connect? For most employees, a broadband connection—such as DSL, cable modem or satellite service—is a requirement for sending frequent e-mails, accessing Web sites, taking advantage of collaboration tools, or getting secure access to VPNs or distributed applications. Some workers who seldom collaborate may be able to use a slower dial-up connection.

As of October 2006, 121 million people accessed the Internet from home and 83 million people used some form of broadband to access the Internet at home (61 percent of the total U.S. Internet population), according to the 2006 Telework Survey commissioned by ITAC from the Dieringer Research Group. Teleworkers using broadband services increased from 4.4 million teleworkers in 2003 to 26.3 million in 2004 (a five-fold increase), according to the "Telework Trendlines for 2006" conducted by The Dieringer Research Group for WorldatWork. (WorldatWork 2007)

Wireless Access

WiFi (short for wireless fidelity), is the fastest growing broadband marketplace component. Wireless access points, known as "hot spots," are being installed in public places, including coffee shops, book stores, fast-food restaurants, hotel lobbies as well as conference rooms and airport departure lounges. Users armed with a laptop or PDA and a WiFi card can connect to the Internet. About one-third of mobile workers

Figure 5-5
Equipment Provided to Teleworkers (2005)

Organization	Broadband	Dial-Up	Voice Line	VoIP	Laptop Computer	PDA	Cell Phone	Printer	Other
AT&T	●		●	●	●			●	
Cisco	●		●	●	●				VoIP for video conferencing
Deloitte	●	●	●		●	●	●		
Hewlett-Packard	●				●			●	Calling card, headset
TIGTA	50% share		●		●			●	
IBM	●				●			●	
Dept. of Justice		●	●		loaner or desktop				Calling card
DOT-FTA	●		●		from laptop pool; employee uses own home PC				Conference bridge
KETCH	●				●		●		UPS, fax machines

Source: ITAC Telework/BC Research, 2004

access their corporate networks from the road by using hospitality broadband connections; the use of WiFi hot spots is expected to grow from an average of 13 percent in 2004 to 27 percent in 2006, according to Infonetics Research. (Verton 2004)

Because WiFi is easy to use, it is possible to forget that users logging on to a particular hot spot temporarily join that network, opening their computer to everyone else at the local hot spot and inadvertently exposing the enterprise network to risk. Require that users have personal firewalls, VPN encryption or other security measures.

To recap, Figure 5-6 presents a comparison of Internet access technologies.

Figure 5-6
A Comparison of Internet Access Technologies (2005)

Type of Access	Maximum Connection Speed	Advantages	Disadvantages
DSL	3Mbps	• Always on • Works with one phone line • No rewiring necessary	• Not available everywhere • Connections require close proximity to central office
Cable	6Mbps	• Always on • No telephone service needed	• Not available everywhere • Speed degrades as more users share cable network
Satellite	1.5Mbps	• Always on • Works well in remote areas	• Service can be affected by severe weather
Dial-up	56Kbps	• Connection is easy • Not hard-wired • Inexpensive	• Slow • Requires dial-in for each session • Shares an existing phone line; you cannot call and surf at the same time on one line • Session disconnects if no activity
WiFi	22Mbps	• Convenient access from WiFi hotspots	• Requires a WiFi card • Security issues

Source: ITAC Telework/BC Research, 2004

Network Access

Organizations have developed several methods for teleworkers. A few of the most common include virtual private networks (VPNs), server-based and remote access.

Virtual Private Network

The Internet was originally designed to withstand a nuclear war. It basically is a network of networks, providing communications services like e-mail and Web access. Taking advantage of its reach and economies of scale, organizations looked for ways to piggyback their communications over the Internet.

The result: Engineers developed a Virtual Private Network (VPN) solution, a secure private network that uses the public network for data transport. Using security measures like encryption and authentication, a VPN encodes the data passing between two Internet points, thereby maintaining privacy and security. Employees access their corporate intranets and other applications via a standard Internet connection.

Analysts at Gartner estimate that using a VPN for remote access creates a 54-percent annual average return on investment. The majority of the savings are from reduced monthly connectivity charges. As noted previously, Intel achieved a 60-percent cost reduction by replacing dial-up remote access service with a VPN solution. (Cisco Systems 2001)

Server-Based Computing (SBC)

Server-based applications reside on servers instead of sitting on individual computers. Users can connect securely to those applications using any device— Mac, PC or PDA. Applications can be deployed via a Web interface, letting users access their company software via a browser. A major advantage of SBC is that it reduces support costs because installs and updates can be done remotely and broadcast to all users.

Another SBC advantage is scalability. When Lehman Brothers lost the use of its building in the World Trade Center attacks, staffers scrambled to find office space, ramp up remote access and deliver their company's applications to hundreds of new locations. Staff who worked from home used a Lehman-built utility called Tocket that made accessing critical systems secure. This, coupled with Citrix MetaFrame Presentation Server for Windows, allowed them to rapidly deploy their applications using a common Web browser. The remote user population grew from 25 users on Sept. 11, 2001, to 1,200 just two days later.

Remote Access

Many organizations, and especially smaller ones with limited IT support, prefer remote access solutions, where the user controls his or her office computer remotely. Some solutions ship the screen images and keyboard input between the host computer and the remote user. Others allow access through Web browsers. Either method creates a clone of the office computer on the remote computer.

Network Security Concerns

Proprietary and sensitive company information can be exposed once networks have been opened to remote users. Because broadband connections are always on, users may be more vulnerable to viruses than are dial-up users. Some solutions:

- Set up a VPN quarantine. Configure the corporate firewall or VPN/remote access server to block users who don't have up-to-date antivirus signature files, security patches and service packs. Use remote control software to download needed fixes and bring security up to target levels.
- Make personal firewalls mandatory. Firewalls come in two basic varieties: software-based or hardware appliances. Software firewalls provide basic intrusion detection and privacy control. Hardware appliances are often bundled with DSL or cable modem routers and provide stronger protection.
- Insist that users follow secure computing practices. These include:
  - Install and use up-to-date virus protection software
  - Operate behind a personal firewall
  - Make regular backups of files
  - Install and use intrusion-detection software
  - Never open e-mail attachments from unknown senders
  - Avoid downloading programs or files from untrustworthy sites
  - Keep applications up-to-date and patched
  - Disable Java and JavaScript
  - Disable file sharing
  - Use password protection to lock down computers.

One would expect the U.S. Treasury Department to have stringent user authentication controls, and they do. The following is an abbreviated version of the main components of the Treasury Inspector General for Tax Administration's password policy:

- All passwords must be at least eight characters long and be difficult to guess.
- Do not recycle or reuse previously used passwords.
- Passwords must contain at least three of the following character types: uppercase letter, lowercase letter, number and/or nonalphanumeric character.
- All workstations, including laptops, must use some type of screen-savers with fixed-password-based boot protection along with a time-out-after-no-activity feature.
- When the system is idle longer than 10 minutes, the screen will go blank and the user must sign on again.
- Users must use different passwords on each system.
- Passwords must not be written and left in a place where unauthorized persons might discover them.

Parting Advice: Have a Backup Plan (and a Backup to the Backup)

It makes sense to have multiple communication channels. If employees have home and cell telephone numbers, "it adds free redundancy to the system," said AT&T's Roitz. "We have even made our remote-access software available outside the corporate Intranet in the event someone is forced to use their personal PC."

Power Options

Power problems can upset the best-laid plans for remote work. Enterprises can usually weather a short outage by firing up their generators, but most home offices don't have backup power plans. Some suggestions:

Keep Batteries Fully Charged

Laptop batteries typically last up to three or four hours. Having a second battery pack doubles the time workers can stay productive. Many companies reported that their workers kept working during the Northeast Blackout of 2003 by using their mobile equipment. Though several Intel field sales offices lost power, sales engineers continued to work using their wireless laptops with no disruption to customer communication.

Uninterruptible Power Supplies

Uninterruptible power supplies (UPS) are designed to provide enough runtime for users to shut their critical systems down. Even a 15-minute UPS window can provide sufficient time to back up recent work, transfer files to a laptop computer and/or save documents.

Look for Alternative Power Sources

Solar panels and fuel cells may provide needed backup power. Portable solar chargers from companies like ICP Global Technologies and Saitek work well in sunny climates. Fuel cell research is resulting in small, home-based backup solutions.

Case Study in Technology Solutions

IBM provides a good case study in the area of technology solutions. IBM has 443,000 employees, 145,000 mobile employees worldwide, and 27,000 employees who work from home at least four days a week. The company saves $300 million a year in real estate costs.

IBM believes in leveraging technology to support employee productivity. "One of the keys to our success has been equipping mobile workers with the tools they need to work anywhere," said James Holden, program manager for global mobility. These tools include laptop computers, a personal firewall, wireless handheld devices, cell phones and high-speed access. "A mobile workforce allows disaster recovery planners flexibility in the event of a major problem," Holden added.

"Telework makes a lot of sense as one element of a comprehensive BC strategy. It should be included as a vital component of the planning process," said Brent Woodworth, worldwide segment manager, crisis response team. He explained that if a company loses a 300- to 400-person office, they can move employees to an alternate center, but it may take four or five days. "Many companies cannot afford to be down that long. With remote telework capabilities, a company can be back in business within hours. Business resiliency tools, such as telework, help to ensure that a company can continue to operate effectively during times of crisis," Woodworth said.

Dispersed workers take advantage of Lotus Sametime, IBM's instant messaging software, to chat collaboratively with co-workers. E-mail is handled through Lotus Notes. It lets users quickly replicate their mail log onto their local machine. This has distinct advantages, Woodworth said, as there is no need to stay connected to the network to handle mail duties.

The company is highly security-conscious. "We use triple DES security. Everything is behind a firewall. We're moving to a single signon. Even our BlackBerry handhelds have security," indicated Holden, explaining that PDA use requires a six-digit alphanumeric password.

IBM frequently tests its disaster response plans and includes people who work from remote locations. "We want to be sure our solutions work for everyone," Woodworth explained. As part of its BC program, the organization trains employees in preparedness and what steps to take if a disaster strikes at home.

Support of Teleworkers

As the number of mobile professionals, telecommuters, or branch office or field personnel expands, supporting these remote users becomes more complex and more costly than supporting traditional desktop computer users within a corporate facility.

Help Desk Support Decisions

When teleworkers have a problem, a technician cannot walk down the hall to fix it. Laptop computer users face the additional complication of working with network connection software, and connection problems are a major source of calls to the help desk. Furthermore, keeping mobile computers up-to-date with software patches and configuration changes is more difficult because most are connected only occasionally to the network and usually through low-bandwidth telephone lines. As a result, remote computer users may be working with software that is one or more versions behind that of office-based users and so, more prone to problems.

Diversified Help Desk Expertise

In most large organizations, help desks are staffed with technicians who are proficient in one particular skill set (LAN, WAN, desktop, voice services, telephony and call center, for example). When considering teleworker needs at their homes, the problem could be related to any or several of the specialty areas. Therefore, teleworkers need a similar type of help desk support, containing technicians with all relevant expertise levels: local area networks (LAN) data, wide area networks (WAN) data, remote access service solutions, voice networks and telephony applications, call-center technologies, desktop computer and server support and software applications.

Knowledge-based Trouble Ticket Systems and Advanced Automated Support Services

As the telework process unfolds, help desk technicians can systematically gather information and track cause and effect information regarding each help desk call from a teleworker. This system allows help desk technicians to identify patterns in user problems and reduce the time to resolve problems and teleworker downtime. Without any prior knowledge or experience with a specific problem, technicians are able to resolve issues by working through the database.

A knowledge-based system also incorporates a "learning" modular technology, asking each technician if the recommended solution helped in correcting the problem. If so, then the solution is rated high. If it was not useful, the solution will be rated low. Each time a problem description is entered, the system will pull the top 10 solutions. This approach proved effective and efficient when supporting teleworkers. It combines different areas of technical expertise into a uniform, easy-to-use knowledge warehouse. It enables the knowledge of each technician to be shared with the entire team.

Automated modules can also be used to monitor teleworker connections and then "react" by paging technicians or automatically logging tickets on down servers. These modules can also be placed within the trouble ticket database so actions can be taken if service levels are about to be compromised. These automated modules provide a useful reduction of dedicated monitoring staff hours.

All of these services, combined with advanced software reporting packages, produce a system that can monitor, measure and maintain teleworker-support services. This enables an organization's support staff to measure response, research and resolution timelines.

Remote Control and Remote Diagnosis Tools

With remote-user numbers growing rapidly, information technology (IT) managers and value-added resellers (VARs) are seeking cost-effective ways to troubleshoot and solve problems for desktop and laptop computers that are outside the corporate infrastructure.

Remote-control software has been used for a number of years—primarily to allow PC users to access their desktop PCs when they are out of the office. It enables them to work with information stored on their desktop hard drives, or even to access the corporate network from remote locations, all through their desktop PCs. While corporations and VARs are realizing the power of remote control as an effective technical support tool, they also recognize that these tools have a high security risk from hackers.

Without remote control, support representatives must rely on time-consuming and error-prone verbal communication between the help desk technician and the user. Many of these business users are not computer savvy. Yet when they have a problem, they must become the technician's "eyes, ears and hands." They must describe the problem's symptoms to the technician who cannot see the computer screen. They must follow the technician's instructions precisely and describe accurately what is occurring onscreen. In resolving the problem, the technician may direct the user through complicated processes that are completely unfamiliar and arcane. If the user follows the instructions incorrectly, that could exacerbate the problem. Some fixes—such as modifying the Windows Registry—cannot or should not be made by an end user. This is nonproductive time for the user. Furthermore, if the technician cannot solve the problem by telephone, the computer may be unusable until the employee returns to the office.

Remote-control software eliminates these difficulties by enabling the technician to manipulate the remote PC directly—without putting the user in the middle. In this way, the technician experiences the problem first hand. This speeds troubleshooting and gives the technician full control of the remote computer for problem resolution. Using remote-control tools, technicians can:

- Troubleshoot problems
- Install and configure software
- Download software patches to the user's PC

- Configure application and system software settings
- Train users (or even other help desk personnel) using a learn-by-example approach.

Service-Level Agreements (SLAs) for Teleworkers

When entering into an SLA specific to teleworker support, consider product management, lab testing, 24/7/364 support availability, network monitoring, IP/password administration, desktop certification, remote installation, reduced response/resolution commitment and reporting.

Product management and lab testing are a necessity in understanding the remote connection to the corporate LAN/WAN and voice networks. Make certain that all products including the terminal adapter, NT1, computer, printer, hub, network interface card, fax and telephone are working together properly according to vendor specifications. Software also is tested to ensure that packets transmitted and received in the remote environment are deliberate.

The teleworker must get 24/7/365 support. The remote end-user in his or her home should get a higher level of support than those workers located onsite and with access to local technician resources.

Network monitoring is essential when determining capacity planning as well as watching for system outages.

IP/password administration is required when establishing and using RAS (remote access service). This service alone usually demands a dedicated resource for corporate LAN applications. When working with telework applications, the IP and password administration becomes *three times* the normal workload and is usually managed by the service provider.

Desktop certification is necessary to ensure that all hardware and software is specific to the teleworker environment. This is to ensure that applications are not loaded on the desktop that could hinder the end-user in the remote scenario.

Remote installation might be necessary for many teleworkers. A service-level agreement must include the availability of installation technicians who can install the CPE in each remote user's home.

Teleworkers usually require a higher than average end-user trouble-response and resolution support. If the teleworker has a problem with the network, he or she will not have access to alternative access methods as onsite workers do. Therefore, the service-level commitment must be increased for an organization with teleworkers, especially for those who always require immediate access to the corporate data. Their use of data becomes mission-critical and they need a consummate level of support.

Reporting is necessary to provide feedback on other service-level commitments. Real-time information warehousing and reporting of all trouble tickets and status of network is necessary to make real-time management decisions for the organization's telework program. Items to consider: asset tracking, network tracking and use, number of users, logistics management for setup, time teleworkers are in process, efficiency of setup, teleworkers returning to office, efficiency of network.

A recommended practice: Negotiate a service-level agreement with clear performance objectives and expectations.

Technology to Support Desk Sharing and Effective Real Estate Use

Desk sharing, also known as hoteling, is defined by the International Facilities Management Association (IFMA) as "workspace that is reserved on first call basis and not dedicated to any specific worker beyond a specific amount of time." (Trenck 2006) Desk sharing allows employees to reserve temporary workspace whenever and wherever it is needed through a workplace-management system serving to manage the operations of the facility and measure space utilization. As a result, there will be more workers than workspaces.

A small staff is usually available to prepare the reserved space for occupancy and manage the reservation process. An online reservation system allows individual employees to reserve office space when and where it is needed. It also enables the employer to measure the use of the office assets, allowing it to position office resources most efficiently.

Hoteling reservation system minimum requirements:

- Allow teleworkers to reserve office resources via an automated system online, with a telephone or by calling a concierge.
- Provide a quick and easy method for checking in: touch-screen kiosks with optional bar-code scanners, telephone voice response units or Web browsers, for instance.
- Provide an automated means of switching telephone extensions so an individual has complete access to their voice-mail services and an organization can maintain its phone-dialing rules and permissions.
- Allow workspace owners to share their assets among many users, measure the use of these resources, plan future workspace capacity, and invest/divest of assets as required.

Accurate data are critical to an online reservation system. Without accurate data, any benefits are difficult, if not impossible, to track. Studies show that without an enforced check-in process, 40 percent of reservations are made but not used. This is especially true of organizations that have tried to implement hoteling using calendar systems, spreadsheets and technologies other than a reservation system specifically built for this purpose.

Accurate space use reports help a company realize true real-estate savings, as discussed in Chapter 2. An extremely easy and quick check-in process increases end-user productivity. And the key to data integrity, to ensure accurate use reports, is a system that is designed to switch phones and make check-in not only mandatory, but also painless to use. Automatic reservation cancellation for no-shows is another key component to smooth operations. Accurate data forces users to check in or lose their reserved space.

Use a reservation cancellation system to monitor and control no-shows. Some features needed to realize maximum benefits of hoteling are explored in Figure 5-7.

Figure 5-7
Features Needed to Realize Maximum Benefits of Desk Sharing

Business requirement	Why it is required for desk sharing	Feature to meet business requirement
Mandatory check-in.	It is the only way to ensure that space and resources are being used and that data is accurate for utilization reports.	• The ability to dynamically switch phone extensions to the correct workspace—including the full functionality of LCD and message waiting light. • "No-show" (auto-bump) listing of all no-shows and no-check-ins.
Easy to make a reservation.	When 50% to 90% of an organization uses a system daily to manage and reserve their workspace, ease of use for multiple users is critical.	• Easy to use interfaces: phone, Internet browser, concierge and kiosk. • Ability to search all allocated spaces or prioritized spaces. • The ability to edit or cancel a reservation from remote and onsite locations. • Ability to see space availability updated in real time on easy-to-read facility maps.
Easy and quick check-in process.	When hundreds of busy sales and consulting professionals are checking into the same office building each morning, seconds make a difference.	• Multiple fast, easy, check-in methods to ensure user acceptance. • Card swipe or scan. • Touch screen kiosk. • Automatic phone response (dedicated internal line). • Web browser. • Concierge.
Automatic and manual cancellation of a reservation for "no-shows."	If workspace is not being used, it needs to be immediately freed so that it is available for others. This is especially important on busy days when workspace utilization is almost 100%.	• The ability to cancel a reservation for a "no-show" through the concierge. • The ability to automatically cancel a reservation for a "no-show" based on company rules and procedures without concierge involvement. • Auto-sweeps for bed checks and checkouts.
Track people, their location and contact information.	People, workspace and contact information is changing daily.	• The ability to locate a person and his or her telephone number through the system dynamically. • Real time reservation processing.
Organization system supporting a real-time mission critical application.	Every employee needs the right space (and related resources) at the right time in the right place—and a way to get it easily. Instant confirmation is required, just like reservations for airline users.	• The ability to integrate with human resource applications so changes made to HR files are automatically uploaded into the hoteling system. • The ability to structure permissions to individuals, groups and organizations. • Scalability—to allow the organization to self-hotel, even as the number of users and number of sites increase use of the system.

Chapter 6

The Workplace
for the Anywhere Employee

Companies with advanced telework programs are creating comprehensive work-place environments meeting the needs of their employees for the work that they must accomplish. Accordingly, these employers are creating mobile workplace environments that integrate information technology with physical facilities at home and at the employer's office. So, these mobile employees are able to effectively work from anywhere.

For the office at home, the employer and the employee become partners in establishing an effective remote work environment. A properly designed home office creates an organized, modern, safe, healthy and secure environment that is conducive to productive, consistent work.

At the same time, the employer's office is being transformed into an efficient structure allowing teleworkers to reserve space at this office when needed for their individual use or to meet with colleagues. These new office designs resulted in companies saving millions of dollars a year.

This chapter outlines the employer's and employee's responsibilities for establishing the home office, and reviews how two companies, Capital One and IBM, are redesigning their offices to create the "Workplace of the Future" for their employees.

The Organization's Responsibility for Establishing the Home Office

Understanding who is responsible for the various elements of the employee's home office helps ensure the telework program's success. A 2000 AMA survey found that 55 percent of respondents felt a formal, written agreement between managers and teleworkers was "critical," while 34 percent felt it was helpful. Overall, 56 percent of the respondents had written agreements.

Extension of the Employer

The teleworker's home office should be considered an extension of an organization, and the organization's telework policy and procedures should reflect and extend the corporate culture to the home office. In frequent- to full-time telework situations, main office design standards established by an organization's ergonomic experts should also apply in the home office. The organization's telework policy and procedures should require that the home office for the full-time teleworker be dedicated for work purposes only and, if possible, be segregated from the rest of the home.

Financial Considerations

An organization must define whether the organization or the employee will absorb costs related to remodeling the designated workspace, furniture, and ongoing heating, air-conditioning, lighting and equipment power charges inside the full-time teleworker's home. The organization must also identify a budget and a clear method of reimbursing the employee for these expenses.

The organization should determine if full-time teleworkers get a standard package of furniture or the ability to choose from a menu of various furniture items. The ownership of the furniture when an employee retires, is terminated or is no longer a teleworker must also be identified early in the process. For example, the organization could provide an allowance of $1,500 to $2,000 per full-time home-based teleworker for furniture, including a good ergonomic chair, and then depreciate on a two-year schedule, after which time the full-time teleworker owns the furniture.

To avoid confusion about who has the financial responsibility to set up the home office, telework experts recommend a company develop clear guidelines about what the organization does and does not provide.

Liability and Insurance

An organization should take responsibility for legal liabilities related to the employer's physical and intellectual property and worker health and safety. This includes clear policies on the responsibility for insuring furniture, fixtures and equipment owned by the organization. Worker health and safety liability is covered in a majority of states under worker's compensation laws and OSHA rules for the worker's place of employment. Further, the organization needs to put in place recommended ergonomic guidelines for the teleworker's health and safety while working in the home office.

The Teleworker's Responsibility for the Home Office

Employees must treat working in a home office with the same respect they treat working in the organization's facilities. In addition, an organization should expect the employee to:

- Ensure local jurisdictions and neighborhood covenants permit the establishment of a home office.
- Agree to establish a designated work area agreed to by the organization, maintained by the employee, and subject to supervisor visits, upon request by the supervisor and with the employee's permission. This space should be adequate to accommodate required furnishings and equipment.
- Ensure that the appropriate insurance (such as homeowner's or renter's) is in place to cover any loss or damage to employee-owned real or personal property; and accidents, losses or damages that might occur on the employee's premises to family members, visitors or guests while maintaining, visiting or operating in a home office.
- Assume responsibility for the employee's health and safety at work, including use of equipment and ergonomic positioning, and inform manager of any problems before they become a crisis.
- Follow precautions in the telework policy and procedures for the safety of company-owned equipment, furniture and materials against theft or destruction.
- Assume any tax implication related to the home office and discuss any such issues with his tax adviser.
- Participate in the organization's telework training program.

According to the 2000 AMA survey of telework programs, 30 percent said it was "critical" to do formal assessments of telework office space and services, while 56 percent said it was helpful. Companies performed office space and office services assessments for 44 percent of respondents.

It is recommended that a company detail the policy and procedures for establishing the home office, outlining in writing the expectations and responsibilities for the employer and the teleworker.

Health, Safety and Comfort Factors in the Home Office

Employees must be responsible for their health and safety at work, onsite or offsite. The organization should develop a teleworker's home-office safety checklist that is similar if not identical to the healthy work habit guidelines for on-site workers developed by the organization's ergonomic experts. The employer will expect the teleworker to perform as well as an on-site worker and thus, should ensure a safe and functional home office. Suggestions for training sessions and for an organization's communication channels include the following.

Physical Environment

In the area of physical environment, consider:

- Adequate heating/cooling/ventilation to ensure satisfactory indoor air quality
- Natural light source and/or good task lighting (from the side or behind line of vision) to prevent direct glare that can interfere with comfort and visibility
- Freedom from distracting noise
- Controlled traffic patterns to minimize disruptions and visual distractions
- Accessibility to sufficient electrical power to safely support home office technology needs
- Safe proximity of electrical and data connections to home office furniture to minimize potential worker injury
- Smoke detectors nearby in working order with a fire extinguisher in working order mounted in an easily accessible location
- A clear exit from the room, clear of slip/trip/fall hazards
- First-aid kit containing bandages, wound dressing, burn ointments, plastic gloves and emergency telephone numbers.

Ergonomic Considerations

In the area of ergonomics, consider:

- *Lighting:* reduce overhead lighting and potential glare by switching to lower wattage bulbs; use indirect or shielded lighting where possible; adjust drapes or blinds to reduce glare; never use bare light bulbs.
- *Eye comfort:* observe the "20-20 rule"—every 20 minutes, focus on an object at least 20 feet away. Move eyes up, down, sideways and diagonally. Eliminate sources of reflective glare.
- *Posture:* hold head and spine upright. Sit well back in chair, with buttocks where seat and backrest meet. Keep "open" angles at hips, elbows and knees.
- *Hands and wrists:* keep wrists in line with hands and forearms. Maintain a "light touch."
- *Position:* find two or three low-risk positions offering support and comfort. Frequently stretch, stand up, walk around, switch tasks or shift positions to release tension. Don't overextend reaches or body positions. Focus on a 90-degree or greater angle for hips, knees and elbows.

- *Alternate work:* alternate computer work with other work using different muscles or involving different postures.
- *Communicating by telephone:* use a speakerphone or headset if work requires extensive telephone activity. (BellSouth)

It is recommended that the company require the teleworker's manager to review the safety checklist with the teleworker. Each teleworker should sign an agreement that he or she will follow these safety guidelines.

Choosing Home Office Furniture

Appropriate office furniture is an essential component of the proper remote office environment. Some basic performance criteria for home office furniture that can support employees' work needs include:

- *Residential fit:* furniture should be designed to be physically and aesthetically compatible with the personal and idiosyncratic nature of the home environment
- *Simplicity:* furniture should have a minimal number of components that are understandable, easily managed by the user, and easily assembled
- *Reconfigurability of components:* furniture should be maneuverable and adjustable to adapt to changing workspace needs
- *Work process support:* furniture should accommodate diverse work-in-process needs including electronic and paper-based tasks
- *Safety and comfort:* a safe and comfortable environment suiting the job's ergonomic requirements
- *Value/affordability ratio:* durable furniture performs effectively and is backed by a reputable warranty and manufacturer, creating a good investment for a company. (The Herman Miller Co.)

Safety and ergonomic considerations to take into account when choosing furniture (BellSouth):

- *Desk/work surface:* glare-free surface with rounded corners and proper height for the work function. Teleworker should avoid leaning on hard surfaces or sharp edges. The work surface should be large enough for computer components, reference materials, communications devices and files.
- *Chair:* should be height adjustable and provide sufficient lower-back support. Keep back supported, knees at hip level or slightly lower, and feet flat on floor or footrest. For computer use, arms should be adjustable as well. The chair is the most critical ergonomic item in any office environment.
- *Keyboard:* should be adjustable for angle and height. Should be low enough

so arms hang loosely, forearms are parallel to the floor or slightly lower, and wrists are straight when keyboarding or using a mouse.

- *Monitor:* should be adjustable to allow for comfortable viewing. Top of screen should be slightly below eye level; viewer's eyes should be 20 to 24 inches from the screen. Add glare filter if needed. Should have front-mounted controls to easy adjustments to size, position and brightness.
- *Document holder:* set holder close to screen to avoid frequent head and eye movements. Periodically rotate of document holder to opposite side of screen.
- *File cabinets, bookcases, printer stands* and other supplementary furniture should be situated so that they store supplies and files safely, within easy reach.

Alternative Strategies that Complement Teleworking
Desk Sharing

The International Facilities Management Association (IFMA) defines desk sharing, also known as hoteling, as "workspace that is reserved on first call basis and not dedicated to any specific worker beyond a specific amount of time." (Trenck 2006) Desk sharing allows employees to reserve temporary workspace whenever and wherever it is needed through a workplace management system serving to both manage the operations of the facility and measure the use of the space. The result is more workers than workspaces.

It is not uncommon for organizations with effective hoteling systems to have five to seven employees for every available workstation. Thus, by applying an online hoteling reservation system, organizations can achieve cost savings from roughly $8,000 to $14,000 per year for every workstation eliminated.

Candidates for hoteling are determined by their "mobility quotient," the amount of time they spend away from the office. While some departments (sales, marketing, outreach audit, inspectors, examiners, contractors and customer services) traditionally exhibit high mobility quotients, all departments have hoteling candidates.

Procedures for Desk Sharing

In creating company policies for hoteling, consider how the desk sharing operation will be physically run and how reservations are managed, especially when space is at maximum capacity. Ask these questions:

- What is the mobility quotient of each employee?
- Can current mobile employees be leveraged to expand the work process to other areas?

- Who has permission to reserve workspaces and in what priority? For instance, a local teleworker might get priority over a teleworker visiting from another city. A senior manager might have permission to reserve enclosed offices. A project team might have priority of a group of workspaces that are close to each other.
- What is the maximum length of a reservation? Are resources available during weekends or holidays? How many rooms can a person reserve? How will presence be detected to measure the actual use of a room?
- Will the operation be full-service or self-service? Depending on the size and type of the administrative staff, the organization can provide teleworkers with assistance in keeping the workspace neat, ensuring supplies are adequate and stocking space with the appropriate files of the individual checking in.
- Does the organization have an organized system of file management? By developing policies on prioritizing files, reviewing records and implementing an effective labeling system, like bar coding, storage needed can be reduced and made easier for the mobile worker to access.
- What resources are to be shared by the functional areas within an organization? How does the organization want to handle time availability of the shared resources?
- What will the organization do about frequent "no-show" reservations?

Change Management

Workspace sharing can represent a significant change in organizational culture. Hoteling is a fundamental shift in individual work patterns that requires successful use of change management techniques to bring about a neutral or positive impact on the morale of the individuals who hotel. With an effective change management program, an organization can help manage employee expectations, reduce anxiety, secure buy-in and ensure the success of hoteling.

Communication, Training and Development

An organization can develop employee commitment by advertising plans and soliciting employee feedback through intranet sites, small group discussions, surveys or publications. An effective training program can be the difference between a successful initiative and a failed experiment. Training should cover hoteling policies, virtual team management, time management and technology skills (reservation system).

Workplace Staff

Workplace staff will possibly include a reservationist and a hoteling coordinator who are responsible for program administration and customer service. That includes daily contact with internal and external customers, either face-to-face or through electronic communication, and:

- Managing and maintaining user and resource data for the hoteling software program
- Making, deleting and modifying user reservations
- Scheduling and coordinating resources
- Providing logistical support to end users and guests (such as way finding, equipment support)
- Reserving, preparing and maintaining designated hoteling workstations
- Generating, analyzing and abstracting system reports for space planning decision support
- Monitoring space utilization, conducting observational analysis and developing reports
- Proactively seeking and responding to end-user feedback.
  Job requirements include:
- Strong customer service skills/orientation
- Proficiency in Windows and Web-based applications
- Demonstrated ability to effectively handle multiple tasks/priorities
- Ability to analyze data and identify improvements.
  Key skills include:
- Superior communication and interpersonal skills
- Positive attitude and high energy levels
- Self-motivation
- Conflict resolution skills.

Here's a checklist of important factors to remember when planning alternative strategies:

- Develop a reservation system assuring space is available when teleworkers arrive.
- At a minimum, provide the organization's basic computer networking abilities.
- Assure that connectivity to necessary systems is simple and secure.
- Provide shared printers, copy machines, fax machines and other office equipment required.
- Provide ergonomic workstations and chairs that have a reasonable amount of space and privacy (no more than the regular office employee does at the main office).

- Design space so that visiting workers may temporarily personalize it.
- Assure that the workplace management system connects to the telephones and automatically transfers worker's extension to their workspace.
- Provide secure cabinets to protect personal items.

It is a recommended practice to ensure the facilities component is complete for the teleworker's home office and for the organization's main and satellite offices. Use a pilot program on a small scale to work out bugs and finalize the policy and procedures.

The Future Workplace in Practice Today

Innovative organizations are redesigning their facilities to reflect employees' increasing need to conduct more collaborative, team-based work. A successful organization is agile and can form work teams quickly to address change. This need to collaborate has become a primary reason for "coming to the office." (Trenck 2006) As a result, facilities are being designed to have more meeting rooms that can be reserved through the organization's hoteling reservation system.

Capital One Future Workplace

One word describes Capital One's Future of Work program: Revolution. (Ratekin 2006) Through the use of mobile computer and communications technology, Capital One developed new activity settings in the workplace and created flexible work styles that employees can select. Note this work style arrangement is designed for the type of work being conducted at Capital One and would not likely apply to all companies and organizations.

Capital One has identified five work styles, each of which has its own office and technology assignments. Associates at the company can select one of three work styles—Teleworker, Mobile and Resident.

For example, teleworkers are assigned to their home office and as a result are provided broadband, VPN and a wireless router for their home. A Mobile Worker also will have broadband and VPN, but will not be assigned any permanent work space, nor will they have a home wireless router.

The other two work styles—Anchor and Executive—are not chosen by the employee. The Executive has a choice of where he or she has a primary office, either home or at the company's offices, but does have all the technology options of a teleworker except for wireless router.

While there are five work styles, Capital One has developed nine activity or workplace settings:

- Anchor
- Executive digs
- Resident and mobile
- Huddle and enclaves
- Quiet zones
- Agile project rooms
- Cafes and lounges
- Technology rooms
- Collaborative.

This workplace environment provides space for both individual and collaborative work involving anywhere from two to three people to a much larger team approach. Space not permanently assigned to employees can be reserved on an as-needed basis. Capital One has created a Future Workplace after assessing the different needs of its employees. The end result has been:

- 23 percent more employees are satisfied due to the Future of Work environment
- 33 percent more employees are satisfied with access to quiet space
- Feedback from peers averages 3.3 hours faster, reducing wait by 31 percent
- A 15-percent reduction of wasted time.

IBM's Future Workplace

IBM refers to its telework activity as the Mobility Program. In 1995, IBM had 10,000 mobile U.S. employees and by 2006 the number reached 120,000 employees. To support these employees, IBM created 252 Global Mobility Centers that have saved 2 million square feet and 7,500 workspaces resulting in an ongoing savings of $100 million a year. These centers have a ratio of 10 to 15 employees per workspace, and the number of these centers is falling as IBM finds ways to use these centers more efficiently. (Sheinbaum 2006)

IBM has created FlexiMove software enabling employees to reserve space and track usage of space. Employees must use a kiosk located in each Mobility Center to reserve their workspace. Conference rooms can be reserved in advance online. They found onsite reservation improves workspace use by reducing reserving workspace far longer than their actual workday. Further, a reservation expires if not "used" within one hour of start time.

IBM has six distinct employee segments:

- *Mobile/Telecommuters:* employee is on the move and uses shared IBM workspace
- *Customer location/alternate location:* employee is assigned to work onsite at customer site

- *Work-at-Home:* employee works the regular work period from home
- *Traditional Office:* employee has dedicated office space at an IBM location
- *Traditional Non-office:* employee works at an IBM location but does not have dedicated office space; i.e., manufacturing
- *Frequent Traveler:* employee has dedicated workspace and mobility tools.

The Global Mobility Centers are designed to support individual and collaborative work needs. IBM's experience is that collaboration mostly exists among teams of four to six people. Accordingly, the Mobility Centers are designed with the following features:

- Provide small, enclosed teaming areas for up to six persons close to workstation pods, equipped with network access, moving meetings away from personnel work areas
- Convert under-used jumbo conference rooms into smaller, flexible meeting rooms, or install high-quality moveable partitions
- Provide small one to two-person workrooms designed for focused, concentrated working
- When demand for teaming rooms is especially high, convert underused office areas or cubicles into small team rooms
- Redesign open meeting areas with more visual screening, acoustical privacy and refreshment amenities and
- Reinforce policies against commandeering small conference rooms for private use.

Capital One and IBM are two examples of *Fortune* 500 firms that have embraced telework by using the latest computer and communications technologies to create new work environments that make more efficient use of their facilities, save money and improve employee productivity. By assessing employee needs and space utilization, firms can tailor the flexible workplace environment that works best for their ever increasing mobile workforce.

Chapter 7

Legal and Employment Issues Related to Telework

Editor's Note: Nothing in this chapter is intended as legal advice. Every employer, employee and employment situation is unique and legal questions should be handled by an experienced attorney.

Many legal and HR issues are involved in the decision to institute a telework program or to improve an existing program. These issues arise whether the employer is large or small, a private company or a governmental entity, a company with many teleworkers or few.

Employers who take an informal approach to telework are exposing themselves to potential management problems and legal risks. And as earlier chapters indicated, an informal program severely limits employers to take advantage of the benefits telework offers. This chapter introduces a range of legal issues related to telework. This list of issues is not exhaustive.

Legal and Personnel Management Issues in Telework

A range of personnel management issues exists for telework arrangements that need to be identified at the program's inception to avoid misunderstandings and disagreements between employees and employers as well as avoid, in some instances, violation of state or federal laws. These issues include:

- *Selection*—Which jobs, positions and departments are suitable for teleworking? Which employees would be productive, responsible teleworkers; and which supervisors would be comfortable managing teleworkers?
- *Productivity and Assessment*—How will the employer and the employee set goals, assess productivity and evaluate the telework arrangement's success?
- *Communication*—How does a company make the teleworking arrangement "seamless" to customers and other third parties; ensuring teleworking

employees stay "in the loop" and maintain valuable interactions with supervisors and co-workers, while also being able to provide the same level of customer service to clients?

- *Work Hours*—For nonexempt employees, how does a company verify work time for purposes of overtime?

- *Equipment and Services*—What equipment (computer, printer, phone, furniture) and services (phone, data transmission) do employees need at remote worksites, and who pays for each item or service?

- *Maintenance, Repairs and Supplies*—Who provides and pays for maintenance, repairs, upgrades and supplies?

- *Safety*—How does a company determine its role in ensuring remote worksites are safe work environments and that teleworkers are working safely and using good ergonomics?

- *Insurance*—Who provides insurance; whether the employee's or employer's insurance covers remote worksite equipment for damage, accidents or theft; whose coverage applies to injuries an employee suffers at the remote worksite or liability to third parties arising from a teleworker's actions? Check coverage issues with the employer's personal property, general liability and workers' compensation insurance carriers, as well as with each teleworker's homeowner's insurance carrier. It may be possible to have the employer added as an additional insured on employees' homeowner's policies when the employer installs expensive equipment in the employees' homes.

- *Use Restrictions*—Ask whether the employee may use company equipment only for business purposes, or also for personal purposes; whether family members or housemates may use company equipment, Internet servers or software.

- *Access and Security*—What is the employer's right to monitor communications involving its customers and other employees; how the employer can review and retrieve any data, program or other information stored on any of its computers or other equipment at the remote worksite? How will proprietary information or products that an employee accesses from outside the central workplace or develops at a remote worksite be safeguarded?

- *Real and Personal Property Issues*—Are any lease, covenant or ordinance restricts in affect for home businesses? How does the employer enter an employee's residence to retrieve its equipment (e.g., after an employee is discharged)? How are the employer's rights to its equipment preserved?

Employers should discuss these issues with employees before the employees begin teleworking. Further, employees who cannot participate in a thorough and meaningful review about how they will operate in a remote worksite may be unsuitable to telework.

Several specific legal issues require consul review before implementation. These issues include:

- *Wage Issues for Teleworkers:* Federal wage and hour laws and regulations may create compensation and overtime issues for teleworking employees. The laws of individual states may impose additional overtime requirements for every worker within a state or for only certain workers employed in specific industries. For example, Colorado Code Reg. § 1103-1 specifies Colorado's minimum wage and overtime pay requirements for certain industries and requires overtime if covered employees work more than 12 hours during any day, as well as more than 40 hours during any work week.

- *Telework and Workplace Safety:* Employers need to review OSHA and possible state or local safety laws as they might apply to working at home.

- *Teleworking and Employee Privacy:* Federal and local laws protect electronic mail and computer-to-computer communications. Employers should confirm how the laws of the states in which they have operations and teleworkers compare with federal laws.

- *Intellectual Property:* From a legal compliance and human resource management perspective, an employer should ensure that its personnel policies about telework, security and confidential information cover the issues related to teleworkers' remote access. The employer should also review the terms of any contract under which it has been entrusted with the trade secrets of a customer, joint venturer or other third party. All these considerations should have their final focus on the confidentiality provisions of the contract the employer requires of its teleworkers to ensure they understand and agree to their obligations to safeguard confidential information.

- *Teleworking as a Reasonable Accommodation under the ADA:* Employers with teleworkers or plans for teleworking should evaluate the application of the reasonable accommodation requirement for disabled employees under the ADA and in the statutes of each state in which they have employees.

- *Teleworking and Personal Jurisdiction:* Determine whether a telework arrangement between employers and employees in different states subjects each of them to the jurisdiction of courts in the other party's state.

- *Telework and Employee Taxes:* States such as New York have ruled that a company located within the state entitles the state to receive personal income tax from an employee who only works part time in that state. Another jurisdictional tax issue is the collection of unemployment taxes and payment of unemployment benefits. It is important to assess the state tax rules for employees who work in a different state than the one the employer is in.

• *Telework Agreements:* Any employer will need to ensure that its telework personnel policy and agreements comply with the laws and regulations that apply to its workforce. Likewise, to the extent any employees who are or want to be teleworkers are unionized or otherwise subject to a collective bargaining agreement or other overall workplace conditions (such as voluntary or court-ordered affirmative action), their employers will need to verify that the policies and agreements concerning telework are consistent with the collective bargaining agreement or other overall workplace requirements.

How to Make the Best of It

Once committed to engaging in a telecommuting arrangement, many issues must be analyzed to make the arrangement beneficial to both the employee and the employer. For instance, according a 2007 *workspan* magazine article by attorney Sarah Flannery, the United States Supreme Court issued a decision that broadened the context in which Title VII retaliation claims can be brought and, under this decision, administration of a perk such as teleworking might be vulnerable to a retaliation claim. (Burlington Northern & Santa Fe Railway Co. v. White) This decision said that an "adverse employment action" is not needed to support a claim of retaliation. Instead, all that is needed is an action that a reasonable employee would find materially adverse—meaning that the action would dissuade the employee from making or supporting a charge of discrimination.

Under this decision, an employer's discontinuation of (or refusal to offer) teleworking may be sufficient to support a retaliation claim so long as the other elements of such a claim are met. This potential finding makes it all the more important that employers establish objective policies by which teleworking arrangements are or will be offered, monitored and evaluated. In addition to analyzing the general policies under which teleworking arrangements are administered, other specific policies that impact teleworking arrangements should be analyzed.

The workers' compensation laws of many states cover injuries that arise out of and in the course of employment. Thus, workers' compensation laws often protect employees who work from home. To manage the workers' compensation issues arising from teleworking, the employer should set parameters in an agreement. An employer can memorialize where an employee is expected to be working by designating the work site (office area of home only) and work hours. Additionally, because a teleworking employee will often be the only witness to an injury, it is imperative that an employer designate reporting procedures that must be followed by the employee.

Injuries at the home office also raise issues relating to OSHA. In 2000, the Department of Labor (DOL) reversed a short-lived policy statement indicating that employers are liable under the Occupational Safety and Health Act of 1970 (OSH Act) for injuries of its employees occurring in home offices. Under its restated policy, OSHA makes a distinction between two teleworking arrangements—those in which the employees are performing office-like work and those in which the employees are performing other types of work—with regard to inspections and liability for injuries.

OSHA will not conduct inspections when employees are performing office-like activities, (such as typing, computer research, writing, etc.), in their home. Additionally, in these situations, OSHA will not hold employers liable for employees' home offices and, therefore, does not expect employers to inspect the home offices of their employees. Nevertheless, it is a best practice for a telework agreement to describe the health and safety standards that must be met at the home office and, if an employer wishes to conduct inspections, the parameters of such should be spelled out in the agreement. Additionally, teleworking employees should be required to undergo training on how to maintain a safe work zone.

When employees are performing activities other than office-like work at home, the situation is different. OSHA will conduct inspections of other home-based worksites, such as home manufacturing operations, when OSHA receives a complaint or referral indicating that a violation of a safety or health standard exists that threatens physical harm, or that an imminent danger exists, including reports of a work-related fatality.

The reporting requirements of OSHA apply universally to home offices, regardless of the type of work performed in them. Employers who are required by the OSH Act to keep records of work-related injuries and illnesses will continue to be responsible for keeping such records—whether the injuries occur in the factory, a home office or elsewhere—as long as they are work-related and meet the recordability criteria of 29 CFR Part 1904. Thus, employers must ensure that their teleworking employees report injuries immediately.

The risks of confidential information being wrongfully disclosed through teleworking arrangements became clear in 2006 when a Veteran's Administration employee transferred data from his work computer to his home computer, which was ultimately stolen. This case highlighted the issue of maintaining confidentiality despite employees bringing work files home or even storing them on a computer at home.

Some actions employers can take to protect their confidential information include: (1) ensure that the proper technology is available to the employee in their home office, such as the ability to work inside the company's system rather than saving items on to the employee's hard drive; (2) limit the types of hard copy documents that can be brought home and require the teleworker to come into the employer's office for certain projects; and (3) restrict where the employee can perform their work (i.e. must be at home rather than in a coffee shop with wireless capabilities).

Complying with Fair Labor Standards Act (FLSA) requirements is especially difficult when nonexempt employees work outside the company because it is difficult to monitor the hours worked by the employee. If the employee is performing computer-based work, perhaps the IT department can arrange a system by which the employee's log-in and log-off time are recorded. Nevertheless, even such a system is vulnerable to abuse by the employee logging in when he or she is not actually working. Falsification of time records can be a basis for termination and employers must advise employees of this, but the risk with teleworking is the difficulty in proving hours worked.

The technology making teleworking possible is currently ahead of the employment laws and HR policies that govern it. Teleworking is still uncharted territory for many employers, but with some basic best practices, it can be a win-win for employers and employees.

The expanding role of telework means that teleworkers, employers and their attorneys need to understand a variety of new legal issues. Using an ad hoc, "let's think about it later" approach can lead to problems. The kind of independent employees and empowering companies who are most suited to telework should take the necessary time to address how they will meet their respective duties and commitments when the teleworkers are working from remote worksites.

Chapter 8

Telework as a Business Continuity Strategy

As discussed in Chapter 2, emergencies take a toll on public and private organizations annually. In late 2006, a PricewaterhouseCoopers Management Barometer Survey indicated that 49 percent of United States-based multinationals "have been struck by a major 'showstopper' or high-level crisis over the past three years—that is a significant event with catastrophic impact to one or more of their major business units or enterprise processes." The survey reported that high-level crises experienced by the companies during the past three years include:

- Natural disaster (flooding, hurricane, etc.) (53 percent)
- A complete shutdown of a major business unit (31 percent)
- Fire, explosions or toxic leakage (10 percent).

Anticipating the consequences of a disruptive event on an organization can be a giant step to eliminating the effects of the emergency. Plan ahead to reduce disaster damage and return more quickly to normal operations. Being unprepared can affect a company's bottom line and its survival. And telework can play a major role in the BC plan.

This chapter explains how making telework a part of a business continuity plan benefits a business and summarizes the key steps for integrating telework into a company's continuity program.

The Business Continuity Benefits of Telework

As telework has grown, so has its role as a BC tool. The increasing number of employees working from home or other remote sites forms a core group that organizations could mobilize in an emergency. Remote-work programs increase organizational flexibility and help companies rebound from crises more quickly. Telework helps organizations reduce recovery expenses and helps boost competitive advantage. Through geographic dispersal of the workforce, it protects employees from potential harm.

Increased Agility

Enterprises with remote workers are more flexible, and this nimbleness allows them to quickly recover from unexpected emergencies. Kaiser Foundation Health Plan, an HMO headquartered in Oakland, Calif., learned this lesson several years ago. A building fire caused Kaiser's finance department to nearly miss an important money transfer, which would have caused a sizeable loss. Fortunately, the person responsible for the transfer had a laptop and was able to access the company server from home in time to execute the transfer. "From that day on," said Skip Skivington, national director of health care continuity management, "we have included the remote solution as part of our formal continuity plan."

Speedier Rebound

Organizations implementing and using mobile technology effectively can stay open during emergencies and, if they must close a facility, are able to recover faster, ensuring continuity of operations. Shortened downtime translates into less lost revenue, improved responsiveness to customers and less disruption of operations. When Intel lost 80,000 square feet of office space due to a broken water pipe flooding two floors overnight, virtually no loss of productivity resulted. Most Intel employees are equipped with wireless laptops, which made it easy for them to work elsewhere—in the company cafeteria, at local coffee shops and at home offices. While the flood shut down Intel's offices for nearly two months, the disruption lasted less than an hour. "Those working from home were already familiar with remote connection procedures, which they use regularly," said Marty Menard, product capability group director for Intel IT. "Therefore, they needed little help to begin working effectively again."

Distributed Human Capital

Increasingly, organizations are recognizing the risks of concentrating key employees in one location. Telework is an excellent business continuity management strategy because dispersed employees are kept out of harm's way.

In 2003, PatriotNet, an ISP based in Fairfax, Va., used telework to maintain customer support during Hurricane Isabel. Though the office was inaccessible for days, with no power or phone service available, the company's 13 employees took their laptops home, connected to the corporate network using dial-up and conducted business via cell phone. (Kistner 2003)

Improved Public Health

Because teleworkers are already dispersed, remote work strategies reduce the chance of employees transmitting disease at the office. Remote work also provides a safety net for organizations coping with bioterrorism threats. When severe acute respiratory syndrome (SARS), a highly infectious coronavirus, struck in Hong Kong, officials at JPMorgan Chase split their workforce employees to reduce the risk of infection. One-third of the employees worked from home; one-third went to a hot site; one-third remained in the office. The company's officials indicated that this was highly effective.

Competitive Advantage

The ability to provide anywhere/anytime customer support increases competitive advantage. JetBlue Airways can attest to that. The airline's 700 reservations agents work from their homes full time. David Neeleman, founder and chief executive, discussed a huge snowstorm that crippled the Northeast a couple of years ago: "While rivals struggled to get their employees through the blizzard and into their call centers, JetBlue had no trouble. Our reservation agents simply rolled out of bed, ready to do their jobs." (Langhoff 2002) Additionally, the company estimates that it saves 20 percent per flight booked by using home agents instead of a traditional call center.

Reduced Continuity Costs

A remote work solution is cost-effective in many ways. Productivity and overhead savings alone allow organizations to achieve speedy return on investment. But telework can help business continuity departments balance their budgets as well, especially if it is used to offset recovery costs. Case in point: JPMorgan Chase has a mature telework program with approximately 40 percent of the investment banking division equipped to telework. By deploying teleworkers to work remotely following a business interruption, the company requires fewer seats at expensive off-site recovery centers. "Without our telework capabilities we would have to invest in far more recovery seats for staff. This is a tremendous cost savings," said Jerry Klawitter, vice president of business continuity with JPMorgan's investment bank.

Integrating Telework into the Business Continuity Plan

As new as telework may be for some organizations as a total rewards strategy, telework as a business continuity strategy is likely to be even a newer concept for most companies. And still other companies may lack a business continuity plan. Whatever stages of development for either business continuity or telework within a company, the basic eight-step process outlined here should be followed for developing telework as a business continuity strategy.

Step 1: Lay the Groundwork

Each organization is unique, so goals of a telework/BC program will vary. Companies cite a variety of reasons for using telework as a BC strategy. It is important to find out if a BC committee already exists within the organization. Business continuity and disaster recovery functions can be found in the safety, information technology, finance and sometimes the real estate departments. Work with the existing BC committee to establish a task force to investigate a telework/BC strategy. It is wise to use the cross-functional committee established for implementing the telework program (discussed in Chapter 3) to leverage the expertise and intelligence of those involved. Decide who should be working members of the committee and who should serve as advisers only based on their willingness to serve and other time commitments.

To help identify organizational goals, the team that is deciding what telework (as part of the BC strategy) will accomplish should ask several key questions:

- What do we want to accomplish?
- What business functions are most vital? Note: A traditional business impact analysis (BIA) is an excellent way to determine this.
- If the program is piloted first, will there be more success/buy-in?
- Does the company want to piggyback on its current telework program, or expand that program to include all or almost all workers?
- How can program costs be justified?

Also, it is important to look beyond employees who are simply capable of telework and positions that lend themselves to telework arrangements, but to the legal obligations a company may have to its employees. Consider the constraints that agreements or employment contracts that may cover the topic of working hours during emergencies ... particularly weather-based emergencies (e.g., hurricanes, blizzards).

Further, it may be necessary to determine which positions must be working in a telework situation through an emergency and which positions will receive paid days off. Be prepared to respond to the question "Why am I expected to telework when others get days off with pay?"

A company also may need to determine and then examine its expectations if it wants a non-teleworker to telework during an emergency situation. Is the company obliged to upgrade an employee's Internet access from dial-up to high-speed service? Does the company need to purchase new modems for its employees because they require the employees to telework in an emergency? What about virus protection?

Step 2: Analyze Risks

This step involves investigating risk factors and identifying how telework can help mitigate the risk. Ask difficult "what if" questions such as "What if we lost our headquarters building for six months?" or "What if transportation infrastructure losses keep employees away from our building for several days?" List potential emergencies that could happen in the local area. Identify potential points of failure that could disrupt operations. Consider such factors as historical, location specific, regional, industry-specific and technological.

Once possible risks are identified, calculate the impact of those risks by determining the dollar cost of outages. This will help determine what should be reasonably protected against and help the organization justify the expense of mitigation. An organization may need the help of a BC planning consultant to conduct a risk assessment.

Scenario planning is a key activity to identify how telework can help mitigate risk. Experts advise organizations to concentrate on three main scenarios—loss of workspace, loss of technology and loss of staff—and focus on the effects rather than the causes of a business interruption.

Flexible work arrangements help to protect human resources and keep vital business processes going during times of crisis. Making flexible work arrangements a part of each of these scenarios will help protect human resources and keep vital business processes going during times of crisis.

Step 3: Identify Key Resources

Take stock of current resources and develop a list of resources needed for a BC/telework solution. Many resources required for a successful telework/business continuity solution may already be in place in the organization. To locate them, assess the staff, mobile equipment, support services, training and facilities. Keep in mind that if the computer systems are down, vendors who are off-site will need to play an important role from providing backup data to providing host computer facilities. Those vendors may need time to become operational. Further, if product is located with vendors, those vendors may be able to provide customer service and order fulfillment. So employees may not be teleworking from home but from vendor home offices or even warehouse facilities.

After completing the company's resource assessment, put the findings (resources already in place and resource needs) into a matrix or other decision-making tool to begin to develop cost models and decision models.

Expectations of the staff may be spelled out in job descriptions or at annual performance reviews. Relying entirely on the goodwill of employees may be insufficient to effectively apply telework and carry forward a BC plan. Keep in mind that the term "professional" has various meanings to various people.

Step 4: Consider Costs

Identify the cost of implementing a telework solution versus the cost of housing essential employees in workplace-recovery centers. Assemble the cost information, develop a budget and present a business case to management. When the costs of running a telework program are compared to those of a dedicated recovery space, telework wins every time—particularly if the telework program is already cost justified from the other benefits discussed in Chapters 1 and 2.

Step 5: Decide on Direction

Once risks, telework solutions, resources and costs are identified, decide on one or more specific telework/BC plans. Organize information into decision models and prioritize them based on factors such as costs, mission, availability of options, needs and organization culture. The cross-functional workgroup should make this decision based on the information the telework champion(s) accumulated and the nature and functioning of the organization.

Step 6: Develop Procedures

Teleworkers constitute a core group that an organization could mobilize in an emergency. Many organizations do this ad hoc, telling employees to work at home during a disruptive event. Formalizing procedures produces better results.

An organization may already have a formal, comprehensive telework policy. In most cases, however, these policies do not address emergency conditions. To amend a policy to include procedures for handling emergency events be sure to include the following points:
- Security instructions
- Emergency alerts
- Expectations for different/reduced workloads
- Expectations for help desk support
- Reduced time on the network
- Prioritized access

- Software updates
- Frequency of telework.

In addition, a communication plan should be developed. Communication is crucial during an emergency, but don't count on having a full complement of communications options available. Among the things that can go wrong:

- The pager network may not work
- The phone system may stop forwarding calls
- The cell phone system may go down
- Telephone circuits overload (if power is lost, telephones needing electricity also will be unusable).

Communication is critical when dealing with a dispersed workforce. Use a variety of means: emergency Web sites, instant messaging, private chat rooms, Web conferencing, collaborative software and e-mail. Don't rely on one method of communication!

Step 7: Sell the Plan

As is the case with a telework program, it is critical to obtain senior management buy-in for telework as a business continuity strategy. Obtaining buy-in may be difficult as many executives do not have BC as a top priority. Keep in mind the words of Miles Everson, partner, PricewaterhouseCoopers' Advisory practice who in late 2006 while commenting on a survey said that, "It appears that crisis preparedness is a topic most executives would prefer not to discuss. There's almost a sense of denial that a crisis might occur. About half of those surveyed experienced a major crisis in the past three years, but only one-quarter expect that one may occur over the next three. And most are only moderately concerned about their company's preparedness." (PricewaterhouseCoopers 2006)

Getting buy-in can be greatly facilitated by creating a one-page overview of the key benefits of telework as they relate to business continuity planning and disaster recovery. Attach a business case to cost justify the program and include examples of successful organizations that have used telework as a tool in their continuity plans. Additionally, the following key points can strengthen your proposal:

- Telework can play a vital role in BC plans. It increases business resiliency by decentralizing and dispersing employees away from the geographic point that is the source of the business interruption.
- Remote work solutions reduce the cost of recovery. Leverage remote work solutions to avoid excessive recovery site expenses.
- Staff can cope with family needs during a crisis and still get work done.

- Dispersing the workforce reduces exposure to common risks.
- Trained teleworkers know how to work from multiple locations and to use the technology necessary to access the information needed for real productivity. Therefore, the time required for returning to productive work can be measured in hours or days rather than weeks or months.
- Telework ensures that employees can get to work when transit systems fail as a result of weather or other factors.

Step 8: Test and Maintain Readiness

Any company's plan is only as good as it is when practiced. If no one knows about it, it's just an expensive bookend. Instead, the keys to success include testing and continuous improvement.

Put the remote work plan through its paces. Experts say the more realistic the test, the better the exercise. Tests help to develop staff confidence and reduce the possibility of panic. No one wants a business interruption to be the first time that employees implement the BC plan. Organizations employ a variety of exercises:

- Tabletop exercise: Hold a meeting to discuss team responsibilities and how to react to specific emergency scenarios.
- Walk-through drill: Major players in the implementation of a BC plan need to act out what they would do in an emergency.
- Functional exercise: Test specific aspects of a plan. Examples: medical triage, emergency notification, emergency warning system.
- Evacuation: Leave the building. Employees walk along planned and alternate evacuation routes to designated meeting places.

Regardless of the stage of development for either telework or business continuity, following these eight steps will better ensure an application of telework as a business continuity strategy will be successful.

References

Alliance for Work-Life Progress. 2005a. *Categories of Work-Life Effectiveness: 5.*

Alliance for Work-Life Progress. 2005b. *Categories of Work-Life Effectiveness: 6.*

AMA/ITAC. 2000. Survey on Telework. New York, N.Y.: American Management Association and Washington, D.C.: International Telework Association and Council.

American Broadcasting Companies Inc. 2002. "Wall Street Takes 'Be Prepared' Motto as Its Own" (network news broadcast). Sept. 6.

AT&T and the Economist Intelligence Unit. 2004. "AT&T Point of View—The Remote Working Revolution" (white paper). Nov. 24.

BellSouth, "The Telecommuter's Safety Checklist."

Best Workplaces for Commuters 2006, BWC National Benefits and Related Facts, October.

Brostek, Dan. 2006a. WorldatWork/ITAC Telework Conference: Telework for Organizational Performance. Slides 8 and 9, Sept. 26, 2006.

Brostek, Dan. 2006b. WorldatWork/ITAC Telework Conference: Telework for Organizational Performance. Slide 10, Sept. 26, 2006.

Burnell, John. 2002. "Lock It or Lose It." *Mobile Enterprise*, Oct.1.

BusinessWeek. 2006. "Smashing The Clock," http://www.businessweek.com/print/magazine/content/06_50/b4013001.htm?chan=gl. Dec. 11.

Cellular Telecommunications & Internet Association (CTIA). 2006. "Wireless Quick Facts." September.

Cendant. 2005. Cendant Mobility Nomination for AWLP 2005 Work-Life Award.

Cerullo, Virginia and Michael J. Cerullo. 2004. "Business Continuity Planning: A Comprehensive Approach." *Information Systems Management*. Summer.

Cisco Systems Inc. 2001. "Virtual Private Networks: How Companies Are

Cutting Costs and Improving Productivity, Communications, and Network Management." Survey conducted by Gartner/Griggs-Anderson. Fall.

Contingency Planning Research Survey, quoted by Brendan B. Read. 2003. "Planning for the Inevitable" *Call Center*, September.

http://www.callcentermagazine.com/shared/article/showIssue.jhtml?site_sectio n=165&site_article_type=23&year=2003&month=9 <http://www.callcenter-magazine.com/shared/article/showIssue.jhtml?site_section=165&site_artic le_type=23&year=2003&month=9>.

Crane, John R. 2003. "Doing their homework." *Denver Business Journal.* May 16, 2003. http://denver.bizjournals.com/denver/stories/2003/05/19/smallb1.html.

The Daily Yomiuri. 2004. "Cell Phone Message Board to Be Extended for Disasters." Nov. 24.

DeLay, N. and M. LoVerde. 2003. "Impact of informal telecommuting on employee attitudes: A survey of employee attitudes in a Midwest pharmaceutical company. "Teleworking: Breaking the Myths" symposium. Conducted at the annual conference of the Society for Industrial-Organizational Psychologists. Orlando, Fla.

Du Mont, Stephen R. 2004. "Beneficial or Critical? The Heightened Need for Telework Opportunities in the Post-9/11 World." Testimony before the U.S. House Committee on Government Reform. July 8. http://reform.house.gov/UploadedFiles/Cisco%20-%20DuMont%20Testimony.pdf.

Federal Bureau of Investigation (FBI) and Computer Security Institute. 2003. *Computer Crime & Security Survey.*

Fetterman, Mindy. 2005. "Retirees back at work, with flexibility." *USA Today.* June 9, 2005, B.5.

Flannery, Sarah. 2007. "Telecommuting: Issues to Consider When Your Employees Take the Office Home." *workspan.* April: 58-60, 62.

Freudenheim, Milt. 2005. "More help wanted: Older workers please apply." *The New York Times.* March 23, 2005.

Gartner Inc. 2001. "Benefits and TCO of Notebook Computing" (white paper). Commissioned by Intel Corporation. July 19.

The Herman Miller Co.

IDC. 2004, "Security Surpasses Cost-Control As Top IT Challenge, IDC Survey Finds" (press release). July 26.

International Telework Association & Council (ITAC). 2005, "Exploring Telework as a Business Continuity Strategy," 2005: Executive Summary.

International Telework Association & Council (ITAC). 2002. "Telework Comes of Age with Broadband." *Telework America Survey.*

Kistner, Toni. 2003. "One Smart Contingency Plan." *Network World.* Oct. 6.

Langhoff, June. 2002. "Virtual Call Centers Boost the Bottom Line." (case study). http://www.databasesystemscorp.com/tech-virtual-call_center35.htm.

Laycock, Angelina B. 2006. "Middle Managers: A Key Link to successful Work-Life Initiatives." *WorldatWork Journal.* Fourth Quarter: 64.

Maselli, Jennifer and Antone Gonsalves. 2001. "Suspended Air: Terrorist Attacks Force Airlines to Restructure IT Priorities and Revamp Plans." *InformationWeek.* Sept. 24.

Monster.com. 2006. "A Changing Landscape: The Effect of Age, Gender and Ethnicity on Career Decisions."

Opinion Research Company. 2004. "Disaster Planning in the Private Sector: A Post-9/11 Look at the State of Business Continuity Planning in the U.S." Report commissioned by AT&T and Partnership for Public Warning.

Pew Internet and American Life Project. 2004. "How Americans Use Instant Messaging." Survey conducted by Princeton Survey Research Associates. Sept.1. www.pewinternet.org/pdfs/PIP_Instantmessage_Report.pdf.

Pointsec Mobile Technologies. 2004. *Mobile Vulnerability Survey of 2004.* Sept. 1.

PricewaterhouseCoopers. 2006. Press release "Nearly Half of U.S. Multinational Struck by Crisis in Past 3 Years PricewaterhouseCoopers Survey Finds." http://www.barometersurveys.com/production/barsurv.nsf/vwAllNewsByDocID /865270A1E53CD90285257249004B4175. Viewed: Dec. 27, 2006

Ratekin, Joel. 2006. "The Future of Work at Capital One." WorldatWork/ITAC Telework Conference Telework for Organizational Performance.

Regan, Keith. 2004. "Instant Messaging Creates Security Headaches for Enterprises." *Security Wire Perspectives.* March 8.

Rendon, Jim. 2004. "Gartner: PDAs Getting Cheaper to Buy, Manage." SearchMobileComputing. April 27. http://searchmobilecomputing.techtarget. com/qna/0,289202,sid40_gci961528,00.html.

Robison, Jennifer. 2006. "Getting the Most Out of Remote Workers," *Gallup Management Journal*. June 8, 2006.

Ruskin, Liz. 2004. "Alaska Senators and Their Staffs Find Alternate Places to Work." *Anchorage Daily News*. Feb. 4.

Safeware Insurance Group. 2001. *2001 PC Loss Survey*.

Sheinbaum, Scott A. 2006. "The Metrics of Telework—Show Me the Money."

Sinrod, Eric. 2003. "Serious Data Loss from Missing PDAs Poses Threat." *USA Today*. Aug. 21.

Trenck, Robert P. 2006. "Why Hotel? Add More People, Not More Real Estate."

Troni, Federica and Leslie Fiering. 2003. "Notebook TCO Comparison: Day Extenders vs. Traveling Workers." Gartner Inc. Oct. 8.

Veritas Software Corporation. 2004. "The VERITAS Disaster Recovery Research 2004" (executive summary). Research conducted by Dynamic Markets Ltd. http://eval.veritas.com/mktginfo/products/White_Papers/High_Availability/dynamic_markets_executive_summary.pdf.

Verive, Jennifer and Nancy deLay. 2006. "Measuring Telework ROI: Metrics Based on the Employee Life Cycle," *WorldatWork Journal*, Second Quarter: 6-15.

Verton, Dan. 2004. "For Wall Street, 9/11 Lessons Three Years in the Making." *Computerworld*. Sept. 8.

Weiss, Todd R. 2004. "Groove Touts Performance, Usability in Updated Virtual Office." *Computerworld*. July 8.

Wolf, Martin. 2006. "Integration Marches Onward Despite Growth in Imbalances." *The Economist*. Jan. 25, 2006: 1.

WFC Resources. 2006. Work and Family NewsBrief, July 2006: 1.

WFC Resources. 2006. Work Family Trend Report, April 2006: 2.

WFD Consulting, 2002. *When the Workplace Is Many Places: The Extent and Nature of Offsite Work Today*. A report on a survey conducted by Harris Interactive: 1.

WorldatWork. 2007. *The WorldatWork Handbook of Compensation, Benefits & Total Rewards*. Scottsdale, Ariz.: 745.

WorldatWork. 2007. "Telework Trendlines for 2006." A report by WorldatWork based on data collected by The Dieringer Research Group.

WorldatWork. 2005. *Exploring Telework as a Business Continuity Strategy.* Scottsdale, Ariz.: WorldatWork.

WorldatWork/ITAC Telework Conference: Telework for Organizational Performance.

WorldatWork Newsline. 2007. "Remote Work Becoming more Commonplace." www.worldatwork.org. Viewed: April 10, 2007.

Yoh Press Release. Oct. 3, 2006: 2.

ZDNet. 2006. "IT Facts." CNET Networks Inc. San Francisco. www.itfacts.biz/index.php?id=P2667.

Glossary of Terms

Business center. See: Office suite.

Business continuity (BC). Ability of an organization to continue operating and provide service to customers when the organization has suffered a disaster.

Business continuity planning (BCP). The process of developing advanced arrangements and procedures allowing organizations to respond to events so that critical business functions can continue with minimum interruption.

Central office. The main building where employees from the same unit or department work. Also called corporate, traditional and regional office. Usually located in major metropolitan area, it provides space for face-to-face meetings with managers and peers and fulfills the traditional concept of an office.

Flexible work arrangements. Any one of a variety of alternatives providing employees with options to meet work requirements through nontraditional scheduling (e.g. telework, telecommuting, compressed workweek, job sharing, part-time, etc.)

Free address. Multiple offices or workspaces shared by individuals on a first-come, first-served basis. Free addressing usually hinders employee productivity because it requires an individual to hunt for a space, locate files and get equipment to work correctly.

Hoteling. Work space system that is not dedicated to any specific worker, but is reserved on a first-call basis. Typically, an online system will handle reservations and reprogram telephones. A small staff is usually available to prepare the reserved space for occupancy and manage the reservation process.

Human resource management (HRM). A comprehensive set of management practices ensuring the organization has a workforce that will allow it to achieve business goals and compete successfully. HRM practices are important when: planning a new, remote-work program, implementing such a program and evaluating the program's success.

Job analysis. Also referred to as competency modeling. The practice of identifying the knowledge, skills, abilities and other factors required to perform the job successfully.

Moteling. The practice of sharing office space among many individuals by taking reservations for the current day upon check-in. A simple version of hoteling.

Office suite. Also called business center. Operated by a commercial provider, such an office is leased, along with professional support services, to companies on a temporary or permanent basis. Typical support services include high-speed Internet access, receptionist, administrative support, conference room and video conferencing.

Performance appraisal. Any system of determining how well an individual employee has preformed during a period of time, frequently used as a basis for determining merit increases.

Remote office. Also called telework office. Run by the employer, a remote office is usually located outside of major metropolitan areas and allows employees to avoid long commutes. The building is equipped with standard IT applications and services and provides a way to keep in touch with the central office. Different than a branch office, a remote office is not fully staffed nor is it departmentally organized.

Shared space. System for two or more employees to share a single assigned workspace and work tools either simultaneously or on different shifts/schedules.

Telecenter. Telecenters operate independently, charge a fee for use of a workstation and equipment, are staffed with a director and are used by numerous employers. Some are open 24/7 with security access. Many companies and government agencies are finding it makes sense to use telecenters to reduce commute times for employees and help alleviate city traffic and parking congestion problems.

Telecommute. To either periodically or regularly perform work for one's employers from home.

Telework. To perform all of one's work from any remote location either from an outside employer or through self-employment.

Telework office. See: Remote office.

Total rewards. The monetary and non-monetary returns provided to employees in exchange for their time, talents, efforts and results. Total rewards involve the deliberate integration of key elements that effectively attract, motivate and retain the talent required to achieve desired business results.

Value Added Reseller (VAR). Business offering specialized services tailored to specific industries and applications.

Virtual space. A briefcase approach to the office. Employees have freedom to work anywhere (home, car, airplane, hotel) through the use of portable technology. Virtual office workers rarely require main office space. Potential candidates may include sales, legal, research and integrators, inspection and customer service functions.

Virtual Private Network (VPN). Combination of tunneling, encryption, authentication and access to carry traffic over the Internet, a managed IP network or a provider's backbone.

Work-life effectiveness. A specific set of organization practices, policies, programs and a philosophy that recommends aggressive support for the efforts of everyone who works to achieve success both at work and at home.

Telework Trendlines for 2006:
2007 Survey Brief

From WorldatWork, based on data collected by The Dieringer Research Group

Introduction and Methodology

The following report includes data from the Telework Module of the "2006 American Interactive Consumer Survey," a random digit dialed (RDD) telephone survey conducted Oct. 17 through Nov. 5, 2006 by The Dieringer Research Group, Inc. The telecommuting questions in the "2006 American Interactive Consumer Survey" are commissioned by WorldatWork through a special arrangement with The Dieringer Research Group.

One thousand and one telephone interviews were conducted with adults 19 years and older in the United States using computer generated random-digit telephone lists. The data were weighted to match current population norms for U.S. adults 18 years and older, using four weighting factors: age, gender, educational attainment and U.S. Census region.

Data for all U.S. adults in the survey (n=1,001) is considered reliable at the 95 percent confidence interval to within +/– 3.1 percent. The primary goal of the larger "2006 American Interactive Consumer Survey" is to generate representative population projections for selected segments of both online and offline U.S. adults 18 years and older.

Definitions Used in this Report:

- Telecommute: To either periodically or regularly perform work for one's employer from home.
- Telework: To perform all of one's work from any remote location—either for an outside employer or through self-employment.
- Employee Teleworker: A regular employee (full or part time) who works remotely at least one day per month during normal business hours.

- Contract Teleworker: Self-employed individual who works remotely at least one day per month during normal business hours.

Finding No. 1: Employers Are Expanding Teleworking Opportunities

The number of Americans whose employer allows them to work from home at least one day per month increased to 12.4 million in 2006, up from approximately 9.9 million in 2005, according to research conducted by WorldatWork through The Dieringer Research Group. The rise represents a 25-percent one-year increase, and a 63-percent two-year increase. In 2004, the number of employees allowed to work from home at least one day per month was approximately 7.6 million (See Figure 1).

Based on government estimates of 149.3 million workers in the U.S. labor force (2005), the 2006 data means that roughly 8 percent of American workers have an employer that allows them to telework one day per month. The rising trend in the past two or three years is likely a combination of factors, including the proliferation of high speed/broadband and other wireless access (which has made it both less expensive and more productive to work remotely) and the trend by more employers to embrace work-life balance and flex-scheduling concepts.

As shown in Figure 1, the 2006 survey also found that the number of "contract

Figure 1
Five-Year Teleworker Trend Line

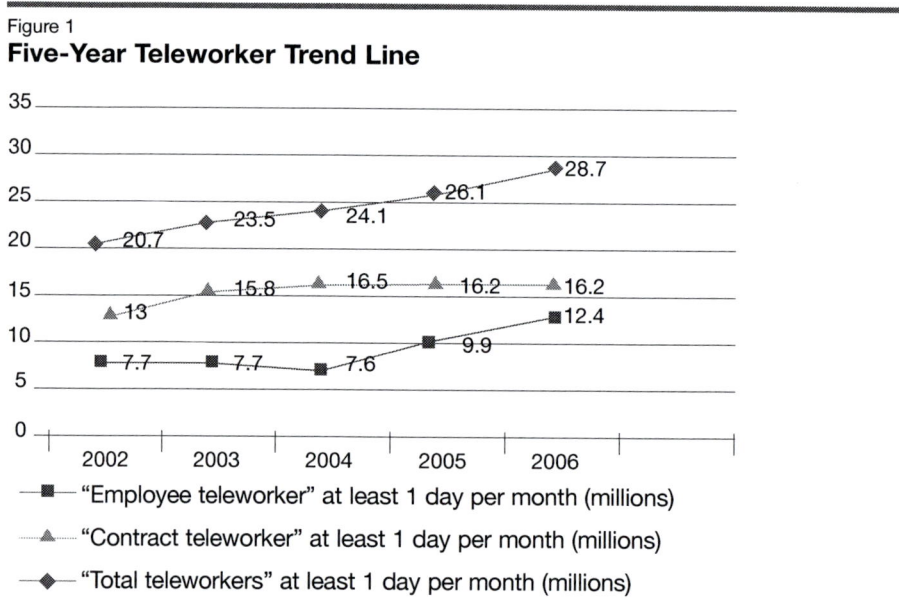

Note: "Employee Teleworker" is a full- or part-time employee who works remotely at least one day per month, and "Contract Teleworker" is a self-employed teleworker who works outside the office at least one day per month.

teleworkers" who work remotely at least one day a month held steady between 2005 and 2006 at approximately 16.2 million Americans.

In total, the simple sum of "employee teleworkers" and "contract teleworkers" working remotely at least one day per month has risen from approximately 26.1 million in 2005 to 28.7 million in 2006, a 10-percent one-year increase. Since 2002, the total number of U.S. once-a-month teleworkers has risen by roughly 39 percent.

Finding No. 2: Number of "At Least Once Per Year" Teleworkers Remains Steady

Other data from the 2006 survey reveal that approximately 45 million Americans worked remotely at least one day during all of 2006. This question was posed to people who indicated that they worked either full or part time at home for an outside employer, were self-employed or who worked in a home-based business. Thus, although it does capture the "at least once per month" teleworker from the previous question, it is using a different time frame for response (during the entire year, not at least once per month). The 45 million figure has been steady for about the past three years, although it is about 6 percent higher since 2002. (See Figure 2.)

Figure 2
Five-Year Trend of "Any Work Conducted At Home During the Year"

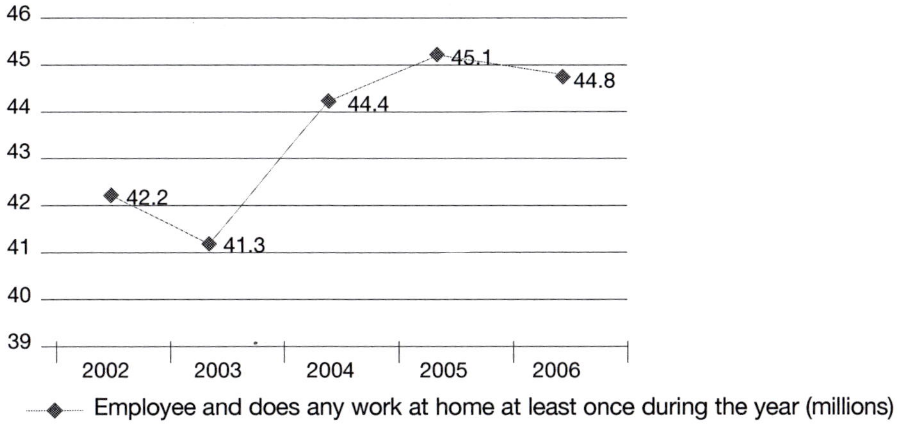

- - -◆- - - Employee and does any work at home at least once during the year (millions)

Finding No. 3: The Frequency of Teleworking is Growing

As Figure 3 shows, there has been an increase in how frequently people are teleworking. In 2006, there were sizable increases in the number of survey respondents answering "at least once per month" and "almost every day," while the number of people who say they do not or never telework at all has dropped by 24%—yet another sign of the growth in teleworking in the United States.

Figure 3
Frequency of Teleworking

	2005 (millions)	2006 (millions)	Percent change '05-'06
None/never	13.5	10.3	-24%
Any frequency	30.3	33.8	+11.5%
At least once/month	26.1	28.7	+10%
At least once/week	22.2	22.0	-1%
Almost every day (full time)	12.2	14.7	+20%

Finding No. 4: Broadband Use by Teleworkers

The number of teleworkers using a broadband connection at home increased by more than 45 percent in the 2006 survey, following an even-larger 65 percent rise in the previous survey (2005). Although these consecutive years of increase seem huge, they are logical given the explosion in broadband and high-speed Internet usage in the past several years. Increased usage of broadband has helped employees more productively work from a distance, especially in accessing corporate networks. In 2004, 8 million home-based "employed teleworkers" used broadband; in 2006 the number is 19.1 million. (See Figure 4)

Figure 4
Broadband Use by Teleworkers

	2005			2006			
	Universe (mil)	BB Users (mil)	% Using BB	Universe (mil)	BB Users (mil)	% Using BB	Percent Change '05-'06
Employed and did any work at home during the year	45.1	25.6	57%	44.8	26.3	59%	2.7%
Employed teleworkers	26.1	13.2	51%	28.7	19.1	67%	45%

Finding No. 5: Teleworkers Are Far More Prevalent Users of Wireless

Because the "2006 American Interactive Consumer Survey" has traditionally focused on PC-based Internet access, the ability to be precise about wireless access and activity is somewhat challenged. To state it another way: the proliferation of wireless and handheld devices has complicated the ways in which a survey respondent may answer a seemingly simple question about their "access to the Internet." This survey in future years will include more precise definitions for types of wireless access.

The Dieringer Research Group projects penetration of wireless access to be 9 percent of all U.S. adults in 2006, and 16 percent of teleworkers. Thus the data in Figure 5 indicates that U.S. teleworkers are about 88 percent more likely to access the Internet via wireless device (nearly twice as likely) than all U.S. adults. It seems abundantly clear that employers and workers alike are increasingly equipped with wireless portable devices that allow easier synchronization of their offices, homes and other work locations.

Figure 5

Wireless Access to the Internet, Teleworkers vs. All Adults

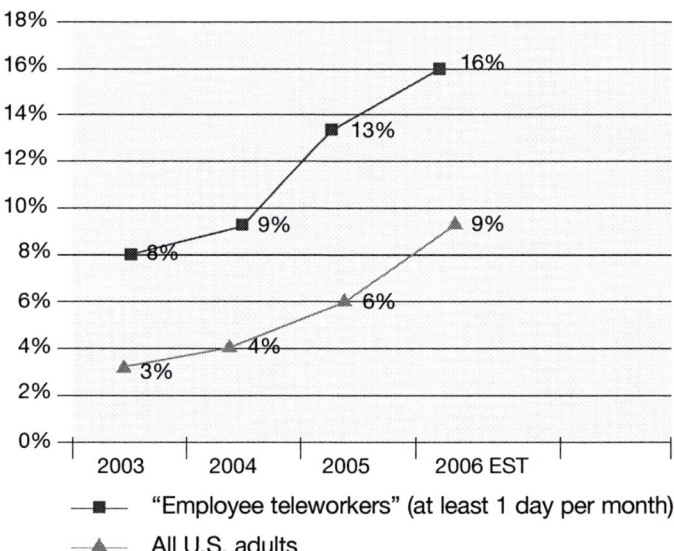

—■— "Employee teleworkers" (at least 1 day per month)

—▲— All U.S. adults

Finding No. 6: Increasingly Working from Anywhere

Although "home" is still the most common location for teleworkers to conduct their work in 2006, this year's data demonstrates that more and more Americans—millions of them—are working from just about anywhere.

In the 2006 survey respondents were offered a question that included a variety of choices of locations that they might have conducted work during the past month. Figure 6 shows the most common categories indicated.

In addition to the above locations, one of the survey's questions inquired about whether the respondent had worked while on vacation. In 2005, people identified as "employed teleworkers" were 4.1 times as likely to say that they conducted work while on vacation as all Americans in general. In 2006, this ratio changed little, so it would appear from two years of data that teleworkers are approximately four times more likely to work while on vacation than non-teleworkers.

Figure 6

Locations Where Work Was Conducted During the Past Month (Millions of U.S. Adults)

Location	2006
Customer or client's place of business	24.6
In the car	24.0
Café or restaurant	20.2
Hotel or motel	17.8
Park or other outdoor location	11.5
On airplane, train or subway	10.6
Airport, train depot or subway platform	9.1

Finding No. 7: Who is a Teleworker?

The 2006 survey provides a wide range of demographic information about who today's teleworkers are. Figure 7, provides a selective sample of the profile data from the survey for "employee teleworkers" who worked remotely at least one day a month in 2006.

The data in Figure 7 illustrate that:

• Three out of five employee teleworkers are male;

• Teleworkers are predominantly married or living with a partner; and

• The single largest group of teleworkers (43%) live in a household that earns $75,000 USD or more per year.

Figure 7

Selective 2007 Teleworker Profile

The "Employee Teleworker"	
Number of "employee teleworkers" in the U.S.	12.4 million
Men	60%
Women	40%
Marital Status	
Married/Living Together	79%
Single/Never Married	17%
Separated/Divorced	8%
Employer Size	
Fewer Than 100 Employees	37%
100-999 Employees	20%
1,000-Plus Employees	38%
Educational Attainment	
High School or Less	17%
Some College/Vocational	11%
College Graduate (4yr)	72%
– Post Graduate	30%
Household Income in U.S. Dollars	
Under $40,000	20%
$40,000-$74,999	21%
$75,000 or more	40%
Refused	15%

Measuring Telework ROI: Metrics Based on the Employee Life Cycle

For several years, HR professionals have heard about the individual and organizational benefits of integrating telework into the work environment. ITAC, the telework advisory group of WorldatWork, broadly defines *telework as working from anywhere* and reports such benefits as higher organizational commitment, reduced employee absenteeism, increased levels of job satisfaction and reduced turnover rates among employees who telework (Davis and Polonko 2001).

These statistics are powerful because they provide concrete measurement outcomes of the organization's return on investment (ROI) related to telework. By creating and tracking these metrics and measurements, organizations can clearly illustrate the benefits they receive from providing and supporting telework, whether it is via a formal program or informal process (See Figure 1). Whether a program is formal or informal, metrics are the strongest evidence telework supporters can collect to persuade key stakeholders to support and fund remote-work initiatives.

Unfortunately, most organizations do not track telework's ROI, whether the program is formal or informal. Fundamentally, metrics are overlooked for three reasons:

- lack of measurement expertise/know-how
- they are viewed as labor-intensive and
- lack of accountability regarding telework within the organization.

Lacking key indicators of success, it is unsurprising that many pilot telework programs fail to move to full implementation, existing programs fail or informal telework becomes the norm within organizations.

Given telework's identified benefits and the challenges of measurement, this paper provides guidance on how to develop and track telework ROI—the key strategic benefits that a telework program can provide to an organization. The paper illustrates how to integrate telework measurement into existing HR measurement programs using a comprehensive employee life cycle model.

Figure 1

Formal Versus Informal Telework

Formal	Informal
Policies and Procedures	No Policies and Procedures (Ad hoc)
Training	No Training
Accountability at the Individual, Departmental and Organizational levels	Accountability: None or Individual
Designated Funding	No Designated Funding

The Employee Life Cycle Measurement Model

Many *Fortune* 500 companies now have HR research functions in-house. Generally, the function of this job is to develop and implement measurement across the employee life cycle. While this practice is not universal in implementation, in theory it is a universally accepted concept. A few organizations have developed well-thought-out employee life cycle measurement systems with measurement tools dovetailing to tell a cohesive story of employee life from attraction to exit.

The nature of measurement is such that metrics are typically not developed at one period in time to measure across all employee life cycle phases. If the overarching model is in place, however, when metrics are developed, the model's architecture informs the linkage in the individual measurement tools. Because the practice of telework often is ingrained within the fabric of an organization, leveraging measurement tools in place, or being developed, is the perfect opportunity to understand telework's impact within an organization.

The span of employees' engagement with an organization can be broken into four phases with each impacting organizational image: attraction, joining, performing and leaving the organization. Figure 2, The Employee Life Cycle Measurement Model, adapted from Colquitt and Macey (2005), depicts these phases and the related processes that measurement during each phase can influence.

Starting at the top of the model, the first phase is Attract. This phase is coupled with recruiting metrics. Once an individual is recruited into an organization, the onboarding/Join process begins. Measurement around this phase of the relationship is typically associated with selection and socialization/onboarding assessment. The employee is then integrated into the organization and the focus

Figure 2
The Employee Life Cycle Measurement Model

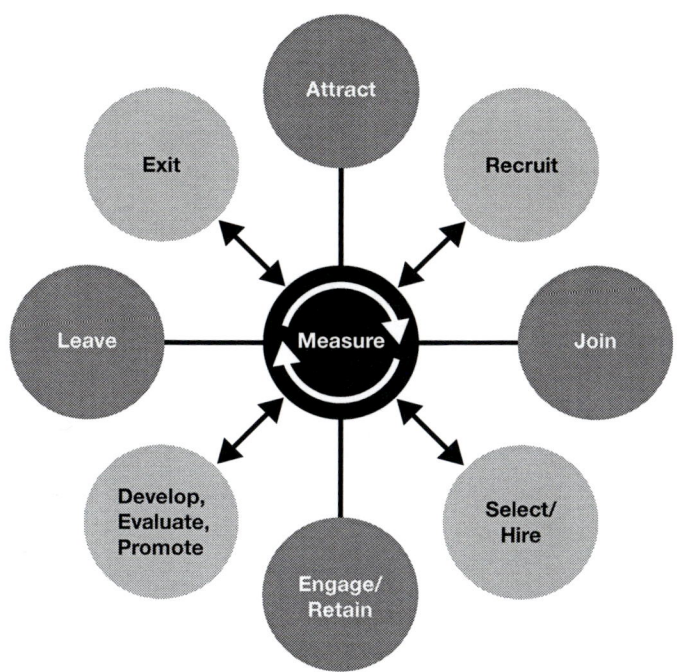

becomes to Engage and Retain the individual, often the most measurement-intensive phase. Examples of measurement during this stage can be from early hire through retirement. These examples include: performance management, upward feedback and employee opinion surveys. The final phase for employees occurs when they Leave the organization. This phase is linked to exit measurements such as data gathered in exit interviews.

When a comprehensive employee life cycle model is used within an organization, information gathered during one phase may serve as feedback into any other life cycle phase, not necessarily simply looped back into the phase to which it is coupled. The circular arrows in the middle of the diagram illustrate this integrative process.

Using a life cycle model to develop and track telework metrics is helpful as it provides a logical framework for examining telework's impact on key organizational indicators. Additionally, the model helps ensure that the full ROI of telework is assessed because it covers all phases of employee experience. Finally, the life cycle model provides both specificity in measurement (each of the four phases) as well as the "big picture" view that is essential in understanding any initiative's effect on the organization.

A Primer On Telework ROI Metrics

Metrics quantify the benefits of telework and, for a formal program, demonstrate return on investment. Anecdotal stories about how some employees like telework are helpful, but clear, hard numbers convince stakeholders to support telework.

Developing sound, reliable metrics to capture ROI often is perceived as an art form. Indeed, many organizations do not have adequate measurements in place because these efforts can be time- and resource-intensive. However, such effort is necessary because the only way an organization can measure its return on invest-ment, or the benefits of a particular program, whether formal or informal, is by collecting specific, relevant data.

Fortunately, the Employee Life Cycle Measurement Model is an excellent guide for developing telework metrics. The four phases suggest not only what types of things or processes might be measured, but also where one can look to find those numbers. Using the model as a guide, the following steps provide a quick "how to" on developing the types of metrics that support and sustain telework efforts.

Step 1: Identify Strategic Initiatives

Metrics measuring return on investment must link to an organization's key goals. For example, if an organization is striving to be No.1 in its marketplace, then good ROI metrics are those demonstrating the organization's high-level performance. Specific metrics for this type of strategic goal might include data on employee produc-tivity, customer satisfaction and product enhancements/quality improvements.

Thus, the first step is to examine the various initiatives and programs at an organization and determine which are strategic. Piggybacking on or leveraging these sorts of efforts ensures that key stakeholders are interested in the metrics that are to be tracked.

Next, consider how telework might positively impact these key initiatives and at what levels. The Levels of Telework Metrics box (See Figure 3) shows how meas-urements may be taken at different levels, from Individual to Community. Thinking about measurements in this way helps develop a list of the types of data that must be collected. With this in mind, move to the second step.

Step 2: Identify the Measurements Already Being Tracked

Most organizations already collect a great deal of data via ongoing events such as annual employee opinion surveys, employee performance reviews, customer satisfac-tion surveys, production data and so on. Explore the measurements the organization already tracks to see if any cover the type of data identified in Step 1. Existing meas-

Figure 3
Levels of Telework Metrics

Individual
- Job satisfaction, work-life balance, personal savings (time, car expenses, dry cleaning, etc.)

Team/Department
- Productivity, workgroup morale, quality

Organization
- Retention, customer satisfaction, positive public relations

Community
- Air pollution, traffic congestion

urements are particularly compelling because they can be used to develop "before and after" statistics to powerfully demonstrate the impact of telework.

If the organization doesn't track certain needed measurements, a variety of third-party sources provide relevant benchmarking data for similar organizations (See Figure 4). Although not as compelling as organization-specific data, they are useful and reliable.

Step 3: Consider Creating New Metrics

Possibly, an existing measurement is not tracking the data an organization is most interested in collecting. In this case, get creative and develop needed metrics. Although creating metrics may be more time-consuming, it's also an excellent

Figure 4
Sources of National and Industry Data

- United States Bureau of Labor Statistics—Household data, Annual Average and more http://stats.bls.gov

- CCH—Commercial Clearing House—Unscheduled Absence Survey http://hr.cch.com

- WorldatWork—Compensation, Employee Recognition, Performance Management and more. http://www.worldatwork.org

- The MetLife Study of Employer Costs for Working Caregivers http://www.metlife.com, click on MetLife Research Center

- Nobscot Corp. Retention Management and Metrics http://www.nobscot.com

opportunity to develop a custom measurement specific to telework.

No easy formula exists for creating metrics. It varies case by case, but two examples of creative metrics used by Wells Fargo (Pon-Gee 2004) follow:

- After launching an education/communication campaign to increase awareness of their wellness program, they tracked the spikes in Intranet usage on the Web page describing the program.
- To demonstrate the ROI of a company-sponsored weight loss program, they calculated how increased employee fitness saved them money through less need for and use of health benefits.

As can be seen from these examples, the types of numbers that can be tracked are unlimited. The more specific the data are to the telework program goals, the easier it is to demonstrate ROI.

Step 4: Link Metrics to Key Telework Program Events

Once the metrics to be tracked are determined, the final step is to determine when to take those measurements. For existing metrics, measurement may occur at specific points in time (for example, the annual employee opinion survey is done in the spring, performance reviews are done twice a year) so, to some extent, the usual timing of those events limits the collection.

For metrics specifically evaluating telework's impact, there are several moments when measurements are taken, such as:

- Before/after implementing a telework pilot program
- Before/after expanding a telework program
- Before/after a key program event (for example, a specific communication, training program, rollout of new equipment, workplace utilization study)
- Before/after a key organizational event (for example, downsizing, hiring campaign, introduction of a new product)
- Any of the previous four points can also be done at predetermined specified time periods (for example, at six months, 12 months, 18 months after an event occurred), meaning a "before" measurement is unnecessary to obtain meaningful data.

It is possible to use these measurement moments with existing metrics too; it may simply take a little more organization or time.

Here is a note on metrics for formal versus information telework. Measuring ROI when a formal telework program is in place is easier as metrics tie to the program's goals and evaluation process. However, it is also possible to provide outcome measures for informal telework. The most direct way to do this is to add a demographic question to existing measurement tools. Doing this enables program evaluators to compare teleworkers versus nonteleworkers on a variety of dimensions. Although one must be cautious when drawing conclusions from these data (that is, such data do not prove that telework "caused" any group differences), these data are still useful and appropriate for evaluating telework benefits.

The challenge with measurement of informal programs is gathering data regarding the investment made (the inputs) by the company to support telework. A little creativity may well be necessary to put numbers to these inputs. Examples of costs possibly relevant to informal telework include:

- Hardware or software provided to informal teleworkers
- Company-funded home phone lines, broadband, cell phones
- Workplace utilization (the time where the worker is present in the workspace divided by the time the workspace is available).

Finally, be sure to get approval and buy-in on the metrics before tracking them. This ensures that stakeholders will "buy" the numbers that result from measurement efforts.

Telework ROI According To Employee Life Cycle

Having discussed the Employee Life Cycle Measurement Model as well as the general process for developing telework metrics, the next step is to join the two. This section discusses the life cycle model and identifies potential telework metrics for each key phase.

Attract

Measurement of the employee life cycle and the impact of telework begins before an employee becomes an employee. The attractiveness of an organization—its image—is composed of many aspects and can be measured through marketing research with prospective employees, such as students on campus. The goal is to assess the viability of an organization's employment offer. In other words, what attracts a candidate to consider employment with a firm? Understanding this relationship enables an organization's recruiting function to build capabilities by attracting the right candidates.

In terms of telework ROI, organizations spend a great deal of money creating a positive image that will attract new employees and retain existing ones. For example, companies strive to be on a variety of "Best Companies" lists, from Fortune's 100 Best Companies to Work For and to Best Companies for Working Mothers to the U.S. Environmental Protection Agency's Best Workplaces for

Commuters. Interestingly, the top 10 companies on these types of lists usually have at least one thing in common, they offer some form of remote-work/tele-work program. They know that offering such programs provides a positive return on investment for their public relations and image-making dollars. In fact, a recent study quantified just how profitable being a "Best" company can be.

The study found that the "100 Best" portfolio, adjusted annually to reflect changes to the list between 1998 and 2004 and provided a cumulative return of 176 percent, compared with lesser gains of 42 percent for the U.S. equity market portfolio, and 39 percent for the S&P 500. An initial investment of $1,000 on Jan. 1, 1998, in publicly traded companies on the "100 Best" portfolio, adjusted annually, would have risen to $2,760.04, versus $1,415.62 for the U.S. Equity market index and 1,387.70 for the S&P 500, by Dec. 31, 2004 (*Silicon Valley/San Jose Business Journal* 2005).

Demonstrating through reliable data that telework helps an organization be one of the "Best" can be a key return on investment metric. Additionally, tele-work is linked to a variety of attraction and recruiting benefits.

- IBM's retention rate among teleworkers is the highest for employees in alter-native work arrangements and is sharply higher than nontelework employees (ITAC Case Study: IBM).
- With its telework program in place, KCTS, a nonprofit company, found more success recruiting new employees under a lower wage structure (ITAC Case Study: KCTS).

Figure 5 presents examples of metrics that can be tracked during the Attract phase of the employee life cycle.

Join

Once an individual is attracted to an organization, and he/she has the capabil-ities needed within that organization, an offer usually is extended. During this employee life cycle period, several opportunities exist for measurement. An often-overlooked opportunity is assessing what prompts an individual to either accept or decline an offer that the organization made. Regardless of choice, this information is invaluable for those functions involved in employee selection/recruiting.

Additionally, during this phase it is important to understand how well the employee integration/socialization process is going. The first few months of employment can determine whether an employee chooses to stay with the organization or leave. At this time, it's important to measure whether expecta-

Figure 5

Examples of Attract Telework ROI Metrics (adapted in part from Cascio 1987)

- Number of applicants citing telework or work-life balance as reason for accepting job offer

- Number of new hires citing telework or work-life balance as reason for accepting job offer

- Number of applicants for vacancies

- Number of open positions

- Readership of an advertisement

- Number of awards, honors or community-based accolades received

- Number of positive media citations

tions are being met and if the employee is feeling like a valued new team member. In addition, this holds an organization to the standard of "walking the talk" and a better understanding if recruiting promises are being achieved once an employee is hired.

In terms of telework ROI, many studies and surveys show that telework options and work-life programs are among the key reasons why individuals decide to accept or reject a job offer. For example:

- A survey on Ernst & Young's Web site (April 2003) asked, "When assessing a potential employer, which is your prime consideration?" The most popular choices were "training and development" and "salary." However, the third and fourth most popular choices were "company reputation" and "work-life balance options."

- The ITAC Telework America Survey found that 39 percent of workers who do not work remotely would like to do so; 13 percent of those workers would consider the ability to telework an important influence when making a decision to accept another job (Davis and Polonko 2001). Additionally, once on the job, new hires are likely to have certain expectations about the availability of the promised flexwork options. Measuring telework participation can thus also provide an understanding of how well the organization is "walking the talk." Figure 6 provides examples of metrics that could measure telework's impact on the Join phase of the employee life cycle.

Figure 6
Examples of Join Telework ROI Metrics

- Number of applicants citing telework or work-life balance as reason for accepting job offer

- Number of applicants declining a job offer who cite telework or work-life balance as a reason

- Number of new hires citing telework or work-life balance as reasons for accepting job offer

- New hire turnover percentage

- Performance review of new hires who telework versus new hires who do not

- Multirater feedback ratings by peers of new hires who telework versus new hires who do not

- Performance or quality review of departments with managers who support telework versus departments whose managers do not support telework

Engage

The third, and likely most measured, phase of the employee life cycle is when the organization strives for the employee to be engaged and successfully performing. Common measurement tools such as employee satisfaction, multirater feedback (360, upward feedback), performance management, and research identifying key attitudes and behaviors that drive satisfaction, commitment, retention, safety and performance are found in this bucket. The ultimate goal is to evaluate, develop and promote employees as necessary.

Due to the rich measurement opportunities during this cycle, incorporating measurement of telework success is easily accessible.

In the area of telework ROI, many studies show that teleworkers tend to be more satisfied with their jobs, their managers and their organization than are their peers who do not telework.

- Teleworkers at Eli Lilly & Co. were more satisfied with their supervisors than nonteleworkers, a key indicator of intention to stay at the organization (De Lay and Loverde 2003).

- A technology company found that 95 percent of teleworkers cited an increase in job satisfaction from being able to telework (Templar and van Zyll de Jong 2000).

- Sixty-eight percent of teleworkers surveyed in the ITAC Telework America study reported that the teleworkers were more or much more satisfied with their jobs since they began working at home (Davis and Polonko 2001).

Research also demonstrated that teleworkers tend to outperform their nonteleworking peers:

- AT&T estimated that the productivity of teleworking employees increased from 15 percent to 20 percent as a result of enhanced morale, fewer meetings and fewer interruptions (Lusk 2002).
- Merrill Lynch estimates that in one year, each telecommuter saved it $10,000 in reduced absenteeism and employee retention (ITAC Case Study: Merrill Lynch).

A variety of metrics are available for tracking teleworking employees' performance and productivity (that is, how engaged they are). Figure 7 presents some examples.

Leave

The final employee life cycle phase is when the employee leaves the organization. Understanding the circumstances under which one chooses (or is chosen) to exit an organization can be obtained through the exit interview process, exit surveys and/or retiree surveys. Once this information is gathered and understood, it can be looped back into the organization for action.

Related to telework ROI and as discussed in the Join section, many job seekers cite telework and work-life balance options as primary factors attracting them to an organization. It makes sense then that turnover among teleworkers is quite low, for example:

- ITAC's Telework America study found that 71 percent of teleworkers indicate that they are likely to remain with their employers (Davis and Polonko 2001).
- THOR, an online travel agency, saw its turnover rate plummet from 45 percent to 3 percent after implementing a telework program (*Denver Business Journal* 2003).

As Figure 8 shows, tracking turnover is the primary metric for the Leave phase of the Employee Life Cycle Measurement Model. However, this may be an ideal area to apply some creativity to processes or data gathering opportunities.

Conclusion

The Employee Life Cycle Measurement Model is a logical and easy-to-use guide to developing the kind of metrics that reveal telework's benefits within a specific organization. Each phase of the model—Attract, Join, Engage and Leave—suggests an opportunity for measuring the impact of telework on employee attitudes and organizational processes. Integrating telework metrics into this ongoing flow increases the legitimacy and relevance of measurement and helps make the data

Figure 7
Examples of Engage Telework ROI Metrics (adapted in part from Cascio 1987)

Engage-Performance Ratings
- Self-report measures
- Regularly scheduled employee appraisals
- Multirater (360) appraisals
- Upward feedback
- Number of planned and unplanned absences

Engage-Productivity Output
- Number of units produced
- Number of items sold
- Dollar volume of sales/amount of commission
- Number of letters typed/documents written

Engage-Quality Outcomes
- Number of errors/number of errors detected
- Number of policy renewals
- Number of complaints
- Rate of scrap, reworks or breakage
- Cost of spoiled or rejected work

Engage-Customer Outcomes
- Support Centers
  - Number of calls answered
  - Customer's average time on hold
  - Number of escalations
- Numbers or percentage of repeat customers
- Number of customers referred by other customers
- Customer satisfaction survey

Figure 8
Examples of Join Telework ROI Metrics (adapted in part from Cascio 1987)

- Turnover percentage of teleworkers versus nonteleworkers

- Number of applicants citing telework or work-life balance as a reason for leaving the organization

---

collection process seamless. Additionally, the comprehensiveness of a life cycle model helps ensure that a company taps into the full realm of possible telework benefits. Organizations implementing measurement around the employee life cycle have built-in learning opportunities that can provide a competitive advantage.

Taking the effort to develop sound telework metrics is worthwhile because whether leveraging existing data or creating new metrics, the most persuasive data are those that are specific to an organization's employees and strategic goals. Using metrics will help clearly demonstrate the return on investment this type of work arrangement (formal or informal) provides.

Appendix C
Telework Tools and Templates for a Business Continuity Strategy

Telework Agreement Template

Employee name: _____

Date of request: _____

Office e-mail address: _____

Employee office phone number: _____

Name of first-line supervisor: _____

Supervisor's phone number: _____

Supervisor's e-mail address: _____

Department: _____

Telework start date: _____

Telework Arrangement

__ Core telework (regularly scheduled)

__ Situational telework (ad hoc, must telework at least one day/month)

Schedule

Number of days at alternate worksite per week ____

Monday: From _____ to _____   Location: _____

Tuesday: From _____ to _____   Location: _____

Wednesday: From _____ to _____   Location: _____

Thursday: From _____ to _____   Location: _____

Friday: From _____ to _____   Location: _____

Worksite

Worksite type: _____ Home _____ Telecenter _____ Other, specify: _____

Address of alternate worksite: _____

Alternate worksite phone number: _____

Alternate worksite fax number: _____

Work Details

I agree to retrieve voice and/or e-mail at least _____ times per day.

The organization will provide me with the following equipment/tools while working offsite:

_____

_____

_____

The organization will not reimburse the employee for the following expenses:

_____

_____

_____

The organization will reimburse the employee for the following expenses:

_____

_____

_____

Security

I have read the company's security policy and agree to abide by all of its measures. Specifically, I will:

- Maintain vigilance when downloading files or opening e-mail attachments
- Employ a personal firewall
- Use passwords to lock down computing equipment and change passwords frequently.

I am willing to allow members of our IT staff to remotely access my computer(s), PDA(s) and smart phone(s) to download virus-protection software updates and perform other remote maintenance, as needed.
__ Employee initials

Emergencies

I have the following types of equipment and connectivity available in the event of an emergency:

__ Pager

__ Internet (dial-up __ or broadband __)

__ Mobile phone

__ Mobile e-mail device

__ Laptop computer (wired or wireless)

__ Printer

__ Fax machine

__ Multifunction device (printer/fax/scanner)

__ UPS (minutes of backup power available)

__ Backup electric generator or alternate power source

__ I am a licensed amateur radio operator

I am willing to use the personal equipment and software I checked above in the event of an emergency.
__ Employee initials

If an emergency occurs on a day when I am teleworking, I understand that I am expected to continue to work if my off-site work location is operational.
__ Employee initials

Emergency Contact Information

Home phone number: _____

Mobile phone number: _____

Pager number: _____

Personal e-mail address: _____

I understand that, if approved, this agreement is subject to all company guide-lines, rules and regulations.

Employee's signature: _____ Date: _____

Supervisor's Approval

Check here __ and initial __ if employee is designated as an essential worker during an emergency.

Supervisor's signature: _____ Date: _____

Sample Training Scenarios

The following scenarios can be used to test and exercise business continuity plans. Thinking about possible disasters and making plans to mitigate the effects will leave companies in much better shape.

Possible Scenarios
• No building
• No computers (host, server or desktop)
• No communications (network, data, telephone, fax, etc.)
• No staff
• No stuff (work or reference materials, courier services or mail delivery, other system or function-specific outage scenarios, vendors, suppliers, etc.)

Using a list of possible disasters, create a matrix with three columns: problem, solution and resources (either on-hand or need development). Brainstorm various scenarios and complete the matrix, showing what your company might do to mitigate the situation. Here are two samples:

Sample 1: Building Fire

Problem	Solution	Resources/need to develop
PBX is down	Use mobile phones and walkie-talkies	List of mobile telephone numbers
No building power	Rent generators	Create list of generator rental companies
Portion of parking lot is unusable due to debris	Require that telework corps work from home or alternate sites	Need list of telework corps' contact information Develop method for quick communication
One floor of the building is uninhabitable	Issue wireless laptops to employees from laptop library Request that employees work from home or other parts of the campus	Create list of computer rental companies

Sample 2: Worst-Case Scenario

Problem	Solution	Resources/need to develop
Public phone network is down	Use wireless phone network	List of mobile telephone numbers
Wireless phone network is down	Use BlackBerry e-mail	Issue BlackBerry handhelds to key personnel
Transportation network is severely disabled	Require that telework corps work from home or alternate sites Require vital resources to telework from home	Need list of telework corps' contact information Develop method for quick communication
Severe building damage, building is uninhabitable	Declare emergency Key personnel assemble at hot site	Create list of companies with backup worksites
Some employees are injured or missing and not accounted for	Activate emergency response teams Contact third-party emergency agency (police, fire, hospital)	List of emergency help agencies Identify employees with first-aid training Employee roll call list Need off-site employee report-in mechanism

Items to Keep in a Telework Kit

Emergencies are much easier to deal with when they're planned for. Advise employees to keep a kit ready for telework emergencies.

Emergency Instructions
__ Contact list (telephone and cell numbers, e-mail addresses of colleagues and clients)
__ Call-tree checklist
__ Troubleshooting instructions
__ Help desk telephone numbers and Web sites
__ Sign-on information (keep passwords separate)
__ Copy of emergency work instructions (which work is essential)

Office Work
__ Paper files/paperwork projects (if power is out)
__ Back up files and media (USB disk, diskettes, etc.)

Equipment
__ Extra batteries
__ Battery chargers
__ Battery-operated radio (for emergency broadcasts)
__ Phone (one that doesn't require electricity)
__ Cell phone
__ Laptop or PDA

Readiness
__ Keep batteries charged
__ Keep backups current
__ Update paper files at least monthly

Appendix D:
Additional Resources

Business Risk Rating Sheet
A simple checklist is on this page, helping users to decide what may be
a threat to the business
http://www.seattle.gov/emergency/community/businesses.htm

CalPERS (California Employees' Retirement System) Telework Program
www.dpa.ca.gov/telework/PERS%20Final.pdf

Emergency Management Guide for Business & Industry
www.fema.gov/pdf/library/bizindst.pdf

Federal Government Policies
Sample policies from several governmental agencies
www.telework.gov/agencies.asp

Florida Business Disaster Survival Kit
www.fldisasterkit.com

Preparing Your Business for the Unthinkable
http://www.redcross.org/services/disaster/beprepared/unthinkable2.pdf

Sample Emergency Plan
http://www.ready.gov/business/_downloads/sampleplan.pdf

Smart Valley

The Smart Valley project involved several Silicon Valley firms, including 3Com, Hewlett-Packard, Silicon Graphics and Cisco Systems
www.cisco.com/warp/public/779/smbiz/netsolutions/find/telecommuting/a01.html

Starting a Telework Program—State of Arizona

www.teleworkarizona.com/Handbook/prototype.htm

State of North Carolina Teleworking Program Policy

www.osp.state.nc.us/manuals/html/telework.html

Summary of Telework Laws

www.telework.gov/twlaws.asp

Telework: A Management Priority—A Guide for Managers, Supervisors and Telework Coordinators

Published by the U.S. Office of Personnel Management
www.telework.gov/documents/tw_man03/tw_man.asp